eating up
Vancouver Island

eating up
Vancouver Island

Rosemary Neering

whitecap

Edited by Elaine Jones
Proofread by Lisa Collins
Interior design by Tanya Lloyd Kyi
Cover design by Roberta Batchelor
Maps by Jacqui Thomas
Photography by Rosemary Neering

Printed and bound in Canada.

NATIONAL LIBRARY OF CANADA CATALOGUING IN PUBLICATION DATA
Neering, Rosemary, 1945–

Includes index.
ISBN 1-55285-453-1

1. Farmers' Markets—British Columbia—Vancouver Island—
Guidebooks. 2. Farmers' Markets—British Columbia—Gulf Islands—
Guidebooks. 3. Wineries—British Columbia—Vancouver Island—
Guidebooks. 4. Wineries—British Columbia—Gulf
Islands—Guidebooks. 5. Vancouver Island (B.C.)—Guidebooks.
6. Gulf Islands (B.C.)—Guidebooks. I. Title

HD9014.C33B75 2003   381'.41'097112   C2003-910250-5

The publisher acknowledges the support of the Canada Council and
the Cultural Services Branch of the Government of British Columbia
in making this publication possible. We acknowledge the financial
support of the Government of Canada through the Book Publishing
Industry Development Program for our publishing activities.

contents

key to icons

 feature farm

 funny note

 advice

 interesting fact

 plant lore

 route

 tour

going to the farmgate

ONE OF MY FAVOURITE CHILDHOOD MEMORIES is of going to the countryside for produce. On a late summer weekend, we'd pile into the old car and head for the farm to load up sacks of potatoes and carrots and stalks of Brussels sprouts, enough to see us through the winter. My city-bred English parents were always amazed and delighted by the lower prices they could get by buying straight from the farmer.

The bounty from a summer's day at Saanich Peninsula farmgates.

Those trips were not just about buying. We'd stop on the way for an ice cream and take time at the farm to meet the animals and chat with the farmers. Once, we even brought home a live chicken, but the less said the better about my father's attempt to behead it with his London fireman's axe. When we travelled, we'd pick anything wild that was edible and visit every farm stand and oceanside dock. I still remember sitting at a picnic table eating lobster in the New Brunswick fog. And when I got a little older, my first job was picking strawberries.

So my farmgating credentials are impeccable, though my motives have changed. Now that huge loads of produce are shipped from lower-cost farmlands, I know I can eat cheaper produce by shopping at the supermarket. And I'd certainly eat less: wooden tomatoes and tasteless greens don't encourage consumption. But I wouldn't eat nearly as well and I wouldn't have nearly as much fun. Heading out to the farm stands on the nearby Saanich Peninsula is a weekly joy for me, from the appearance of the first asparagus in April to the day my favourite stand closes when it runs out of produce in February. I rarely go just for the food: it's too tempting to take a walk on a neighbouring beach or have coffee at a back-road café.

When I travel, I search out farmers and head for the produce markets. I've stopped by the roadside for honey in southern Bohemia, fresh pineapple on the fringes of the Ecuadorian Andes, local cheese in France, cassis in Quebec, Spy apples in Ontario.

Vancouver Island rivals any destination I have visited in the quality and variety of farm products you can buy at roadside stands or markets. No, I can't get fresh pineapple—but, at various times of the year, I can buy fresh figs, miraculous strawberries (plus an amazing range of other berries), salad greens, seafood, even ostrich meat if I so choose. Of course, there are drawbacks: farmgaters can become so single-minded that they find themselves, as I recently did, wheeling into a driveway signposted "Rabbit Parts," only to discover they meant the cars, not the creatures. Yet shopping at the farmgate will always be a delight for me. I hope you find it so as well.

Vancouver Island: The Producing Regions

Avid gardeners produce fruit and vegetables in every corner of the island, sometimes against considerable odds. But some areas are blessed with better soil, better climate and more opportunities for farmgating.

- THE SAANICH PENINSULA runs north from the city of Victoria to the ferry terminal at Swartz Bay. There are more producers here than anywhere else on the island, from long-time career farmers whose traditions go back six generations to hobby farmers who experiment with a variety of crops or sell the excess from their home gardens.

- METCHOSIN/SOOKE, west of Victoria, with rockier ground and more forest cover, supports fewer full-time producers. But it's fertile ground for honey producers, fruit growers and others, many of whom sell mainly through the Metchosin and Sooke markets.

- On THE GULF ISLANDS, Saltspring is the major producer, with cheese, apples and lamb in the forefront. There are farmgaters on every island.

- THE COWICHAN VALLEY extends from Cobble Hill in the south to Chemainus in the north. Aficionados promote it as Canada's Provence—and it's certainly the island's major winemaking region. Berries flourish here, as do many kinds of vegetables and fruits.

- THE MID-ISLAND is a wide-ranging region, from Ladysmith in the south to Qualicum Beach in the north, and west to Port Alberni. Fewer producers exist here than in the valleys to north and south—but, again, there is a wide variety of produce if you look for it, as well as seafood and other specialties.

- THE COMOX VALLEY runs from Qualicum Bay in the south to Black Creek in the north; the region takes in the northern Gulf Islands. This is another fertile valley, with many dairy farms, a cheesemaker and stands selling vegetables, berries and tree fruits.

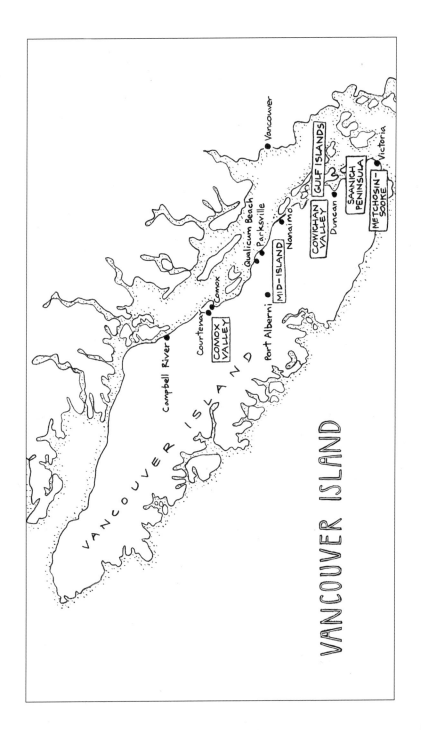

Going to Market

Just about every town or region on the island has a farmers' market, where you can buy direct from the producer. Some are large, some are small. Some maintain a very close connection to surrounding farm fields, while others are in the city. Some allow other sellers—of crafts or art or even second-hand goods—while others are purists, open only to food producers.

These markets are held on either Saturday or Sunday, usually in the morning. A listing of regional markets is included in each section.

WHEN IS IT FRESH?

If you're a supermarket shopper, you probably expect the same produce pretty much year-round, imported from Mexico or the southern U.S. or even farther afield. One of the joys of farmgating is a knowledge of the changing seasons. You eagerly anticipate the first asparagus, the early strawberries, the first newly picked apples, the squash and pumpkins. The chart on page 12 gives an idea of when various produce is available from South Island farms. North Island produce may be a week or two later than these dates.

Who's in the Guide

Most farms on the island that welcome farmgaters are in the guide. Some are featured, not necessarily because their produce is better, but because they are open longer hours, sell specialty products, are able to be more welcoming to those who drop by without calling ahead or have interesting stories to tell.

Most farmgate sellers avoid pesticides, herbicides and other chemicals. If it is important to you that your food is raised without exposure to any of these, ask the farmers: they will tell you how they grow or raise their produce.

Farming is a risky business, one where low profit margins make it difficult to stay in business. Some of the farmgaters mentioned

When Is It Fresh?

Product	J	F	M	A	M	J	J	A	S	O	N	D
Apples	■	■	■				■	■	■	■	■	■
Asparagus				■	■							
Beans						■	■	■	■			
Beets	■					■	■	■	■	■	■	■
Blackberries							■	■				
(Boysen, Marion)												
Blueberries							■	■	■			
Broccoli						■	■	■	■	■		
Cabbage	■						■	■	■	■	■	■
Carrots	■					■	■	■	■	■	■	■
Cauliflower	■			■	■	■	■	■	■	■	■	
Corn							■	■	■			
Cucumbers				❖	❖	❖	❖	■	■	■	❖	
Currants/Josta-berries							■	■				
Emu Products	■	■	■	■	■	■	■	■	■	■	■	■
Garlic	■						■	■	■	■	■	■
Gooseberries							■	■				
Herbs				■	■	■	■	■	■			
Honey	■	■	■	■	■	■	■	■	■	■	■	■
Kiwi Fruit	■									■	■	■
Lettuce						■	■	■	■	■	■	
Loganberries							■	■				
Onions	■						■	■	■	■	■	■
Ostrich Products	■	■	■	■	■	■	■	■	■	■	■	■
Pears								■	■			
Peppers				❖	❖	❖	❖	■	■	■	■	
Potatoes	■						■	■	■	■	■	■
Preserves	■	■	■	■	■	■	■	■	■	■	■	■
Pumpkins										■	■	
Rhubarb				■	■	■	■	■				
Spinach					■	■		■				
Squash	■						■	■	■	■	■	■
Strawberries						■	■	■	■	■		
Tomatoes				❖	❖	❖	■	■	■	■	■	
Venison	■	■	■	■	■	■	■	■	■	■	■	■

❖ Hothouse Grown

Information courtesy of the Southern Vancouver Island Direct Farm Marketing Association in this book may have decided to leave farming or no longer sell from the farm. But there will be others who take over; the roads and routes mentioned in each section provide the best chances of finding both new and established farmgates.

Local maps and guides come in very handy when you are searching for farms and other producers. For major listings and locations on the south island, pick up a copy of the current *farmfresh*, a growers' guide put out each year by the Southern Vancouver Island Direct Farm Marketing Association; it's particularly helpful on the Saanich Peninsula and in the Cowichan Valley. Check at tourist infocentres in the Parksville–Qualicum area for a map and names of farmgates in that region. Local newspapers often contain advertisements in the classified section for what's fresh at the farmgate in any given week.

A PURELY PERSONAL LIST OF ISLAND PRODUCTS
I'D RATHER NOT DO WITHOUT

- A trio of cheeses: Moonstruck's Baby Blue (Saltspring), David Wood's Salt Spring herbed goat cheese, Natural Pastures Wasabi cheese (Courtenay)
- Cherry Point's Pinot Gris (Cowichan Bay), Blue Grouse's Müller Thurgau (Duncan area)
- Regatta's Tribute strawberries (Coombs)
- Mar's Pumpkin Patch's Nantes carrots (Saanich Peninsula)
- Sun-warmed Big Beef tomatoes from Nanoose Edibles (Nanoose Bay)
- Fresh basil from Providence Farm (Duncan)
- Nature's Way Darrow blueberries (Courtenay)
- Flavoured smoked salmon from French Creek Seafoods
- Oysters from Fanny Bay
- Silver Rill sweet corn (Saanich)
- Silverside raspberries (Cobble Hill)
- Cowichan Bay Farm smoked chicken
- Salsa from Arbutus Ridge Farm (Cowichan Bay)

saanich peninsula

IT'S A SUNNY SUMMER WEEKDAY, I'm thinking about dinner—
and that means a trip to Saanich farm stands.

Saanich is the best of all island worlds when it comes to farmgating. With some of the richest farmland on the island, probably
the best all-round climate and a population base that encourages
farmers, every product that can be grown on the island ripens in
Saanich fields, gardens or greenhouses. We're a little short of vineyards and home-produced wines, but a number of vintners are
promising to change even that.

Farmgate signs signal available produce.

Saanich has a long agricultural heritage. Once the level areas around Fort Victoria were occupied, farmers headed out to the peninsula, to take advantage of the natural meadows and rich soils. From 1858 on, when land could be officially registered, the documents record the buying and selling of farmland from Cordova Bay to Deep Cove and the Sidney area. Interestingly, a number of early Saanich farmers were Black, immigrants who fled either slavery or bias against Blacks in the United States. And the area was well enough regarded in the early part of the century that the federal government founded an experimental farm here in 1912.

That heritage underlies today's strong and varied agricultural scene. My own peninsula gathering trips vary. Short of time or after a specific product? I'll probably get no further than Oldfield Road or Island View Road. Looking for the experience of a few hours spent meandering along back roads? Then I will probably end up out in Deep Cove, having stopped at half a dozen farm markets or stands along the way.

For me, the Saanich season begins with strawberries. Years back, Saanich strawberries were sent by train to the prairies, bringing a touch of summer to prairie cities. Now, most are sold nearer home: a simple note in the local paper announcing strawberry season brings out hundreds of people to pick their own or

"

"Whilst the coast line of the district . . . presents a rocky and barren aspect, a view of the interior soon changes that opinion; in no part of the country is the soil, which is generally a black loam, more fertile, or better adapted for crops of all kinds, fruits and garden produce. . . . The growing of cereals is discouraged, as land can be put to more profitable uses for market gardening, fruit, hops, dairying, sheep, swine and poultry production, for all of which it is admirably suited....A very superior quality of fruit is produced in this section by those who give that attention which advanced methods demand."

—REPORT OF THE DEPARTMENT OF AGRICULTURE, 1902

buy ready-picked. Raspberries, blueberries, some of the many crosses and hybrids of blackberries, currants, gooseberries: as much as any type of product, soft fruits symbolize the Saanich farmgate. Then it's on into summer with lettuces and carrots and peas and early potatoes. Beans and apples, squash and corn, round out the season.

Much of the joy of random Saanich farmgating is in the special and the unexpected—figs, perhaps, or josta-berries, or ostriches—or just the enjoyment of reconnecting with the rural landscape. Despite the pressures of increasing population, Saanich still has many farm fields. Thanks to the Agricultural Land Reserve put in place in the early 1970s, much of the Saanich Peninsula has escaped subdivisions, and urban containment boundaries ensure that the fields will survive—at least for now.

The Markets

Various markets are held in Victoria itself, as well as on the peninsula and elsewhere in the area. Farmers and market gardeners, as well as craftspeople and other local producers, attend these markets.

- FERNWOOD STREET MARKET, Saturdays 10 a.m. to 3 p.m., late May to mid-October, Gladstone and Fernwood streets.
- HIGHLAND FARMERS' MARKET, last Sunday of the month 10 a.m. to 2 p.m., May to September, Caleb Pike Homestead, 1565 Millstream Road.
- JAMES BAY COMMUNITY MARKET, Saturdays 9 a.m. to 3 p.m., May to early October, Menzies and Superior streets.
- MOSS STREET COMMUNITY MARKET, Saturdays 10 a.m. to 2 p.m., mid-May to mid-October, Sir James Douglas Elementary School, Fairfield Road and Moss Street.
- PENINSULA COUNTRY MARKET, Saturdays 9 a.m. to 1 p.m., mid-June to mid-October, Saanich Fairgrounds, Stelly's Cross Road.
- SIDNEY SUMMER MARKET, Thursdays 5:30 to 8:30 p.m., July and August, Beacon Avenue east of 5th Street.

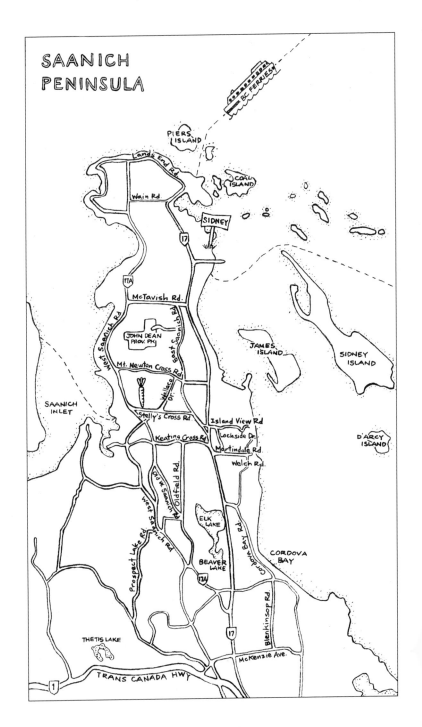

The Route

Almost any area of the Saanich Peninsula rewards farmgaters. Closest to town is Blenkinsop Road north of McKenzie; from there, wander through the Martindale Flats along Welch and Martindale roads, cross over to Island View Road along Lochside, then turn right (east) on Island View. U-turn to cross the highway on Island View, then continue on a choice of routes.

From Keating Cross Road, follow Oldfield Road for the most complete choice of seasonal produce. Or, if you are coming from town, take Old West Saanich Road from West Saanich Road, and continue on Oldfield to Keating Cross Road. Follow Veyaness from Keating for more farmgate stands.

Other roads that offer rewards for farmgaters:
- Stelly's Cross Road and the side roads from Stelly's
- East Saanich Road
- West Saanich Road, anywhere from Royal Oak to Deep Cove
- Wallace Drive west of West Saanich Road
- Mount Newton Cross Road
- Roads in and around Deep Cove

Along the Way: Blenkinsop Road

Farm stands appear and disappear along Blenkinsop Road between McKenzie and Royal Oak roads as the season progresses. You can almost always find a stand or two with seasonal produce, usually along the east side of the road. For reasonably priced free-run eggs, drop into GALEY BROTHERS EGGS (4400 Blenkinsop, 250-477-6733; Thursday and Friday 10 a.m. to 5 p.m., Saturday 9 a.m. to 4 p.m.).

Galey Farms

A giggle of school kids tumbles off the bus and stampedes towards the corn maze. Supervisors corral them and lead them off to the farm wagon that will take them on a storytelling tour of the pumpkin patch. Meanwhile, other kids arrive, by car and van and bus, to check out the petting zoo, the maze, the pumpkins. It's just another

School kids crowd around the entrance to Galey's corn maze, waiting their turn to ride the hay wagon to the pumpkin patch.

normal October day at GALEY FARMS MAZE 'N MARKET (4150 Blenkinsop Road, 250-477-5713; daily June to end of October).

A third-generation family farm, Galey's has long been known for its farm market and for the egg operation just down the road. But from mid-July on, the farm is now better known for its corn maze—designed and planted early in the season, different each year—that features a ghost town, bridges, scarecrows and caves. Galey's also provides a petting zoo, a pumpkin festival and school

GIANT PUMPKINS

Many a market offers you your pick of the pumpkins for a dollar or two—but they're not talking the world champion size. Using seed from a giant variety developed in Nova Scotia, growers all across North America now compete to produce the world's biggest pumpkin. The current record? Some 572 kilograms, which would have a circumference of more than five metres. And wouldn't that make an impressive jack o'lantern?

tours. Phone or check *www.galeyfarms.com* for corn maze and special event hours.

And, oh yes, you can still buy berries, ten varieties of corn and a host of other vegetables at the market.

MAIZE MAZE? IT'S AMAZIN'

In the beginning, there were none—but 10 years later, corn mazes have become the craze. They range from small fields of corn cut through by simple pathways to many-hectare theme mazes that hide treasures, ghoulish creatures and dead ends.

Hard to say just why the making of corn mazes became so popular in such a short time after the first ones were reported in the 1990s. But it's a concept with legs, as they say: now, no Hallowe'en would be complete without a trip to the maze.

Along the Way: Martindale Flats, Island View Road

Welch and Martindale roads provide a nicely scenic route across the Martindale Flats, an area well-known for the huge variety of birds it attracts, especially in fall when birds are heading south and in winter when the fields flood. Some 170 bird species have been recorded on the flats. While you are looking for produce, keep an eye and ear out for skylarks in the spring, pheasants and barn owls, geese and even, though rarely, gyrfalcons. Hedgerows edge the southern part of Welch Road; the fields farther north and along Martindale Road provide a varying kaleidoscope of colour as different crops mature. Kiwis grow at the corner of the two roads.

In season, brightly coloured signs depicting strawberries direct purchasers to the SOL FARM stand (Livesay Road off Welch Road, 250-883-3276); other produce is also available here June through August. In June and July, you'll find fresh peas at CUCUMBER CORNER, (6220 Welch Road, 250-544-4831). Later in the year, look for beets, pickling cucumbers and dill and, eventually, pumpkins. Keep your eyes open for other seasonal stands along Welch Road; they offer a variety of produce from overflowing gardens, including garlic and green beans, squash and lettuce, and, almost always, flowers.

Turn right (north) from Martindale Road onto Lochside. (Take care here: this section of Lochside is part of the Galloping Goose Trail and is heavily used by cyclists who don't always pay attention to vehicle traffic; by farm vehicles; and by devotees of model-airplane flight, whose flying base is just along the road.) Lochside leads across farm fields to Island View Road; to the right and over the hill is one of the peninsula's nicer beaches, well worth a ramble. FIRBANK FARM (2834 Island View; 250-652-0016; Wednesday to Saturday 9 a.m. to 5 p.m., year-round) has a wide variety of seasonal produce.

If you are interested in farming history, make a stop at Heritage Acres, maintained by the Saanich Historical Artifacts Society, on Lochside north of Island View Road. Old farm equipment and area agricultural history are on display here; on weekends through the summer and fall, you'll find such activities as steam threshing and model railroading.

Sunlight dapples kiwi vines and fruits on Martindale Road.

Michell Brothers

MICHELL BROTHERS FARM (3015 and 3047 Island View Road; 250-562-2100 or 250-652-1939; daily, late May to February) is a tradition for many long-time Victoria residents who make a day of their farmgating. The trip often includes coffee at Mattick's, which started life as a farm market but has gone much bigger and more upscale, and lunch somewhere in Sidney, as well as a visit to Michell's to see what's available this week.

Vern Michell, one of the brothers who owns Michell's, says the farm is a tradition in the Michell family as well. Vern's great-grand-father, Thomas, came from Wales in the late 1850s, tried the gold rush, then settled into farming with horses, grain, chickens and cows. He bought 50 hectares from Howard Estes, a Black farmer, in 1867. The next year, Thomas bought a further 21 head of cattle (small and big), 18 pigs, 24 chickens and turkeys, a wagon and har-ness, a plow, milking pans and other equipment from Estes. Vern's grandfather continued and expanded the business, as did his father and uncles. Potatoes were their major crop from the 1940s to 1982, when an outbreak of golden nematode put an end to potato growing for many years. Though you can once more grow potatoes in some areas of Saanich, the farm stand is in an area where their cultivation is still forbidden.

The Michells took a big hit, but the family was already growing strawberries, loganberries, cabbage, cauliflower and other crops, so the farm tradition continued. Vern and brother Wilmer and their wives and sons and daughters-in-law—and their granddaughters and grandsons—continue to farm, now into the sixth generation of Michells farming in the same area. The first crop of the year is lettuce, on about May 20; then come strawberries (they sell 30 tonnes each year). Then come crops such as cabbage, cauli-flower and broccoli, carrots and beets; then raspberries, logans, tayberries, marionberries, blueberries; then into the bulk carrots and beets; then corn and cucumbers and dill weed. Apples from their 2,000 trees finish off the crop year.

Vern's favourite crop? "I like raspberries. We've gone through the

Members of the Michell family bring potatoes to their Island View Road market.

intense period of strawberries, then raspberries are a little more relaxed—and you can stand up to pick them." The worst crop? "The native weeds. They've been growing here a long time, they're used to the drought, they don't stop growing just because it doesn't rain."

Michells is open at one of their two neighbouring locations from May through February. "We sell what we grow. When we run out, we close. When we've grown another crop, we open again."

 Pedersen Berry Farm

A five-year-old swings his ice-cream pail in a circle, then plonks himself down in the middle of the patch. He's here for that ritual of childhood, picking strawberries—though, as usual, the adults pick and the kids taste, wander and ask if it's time to go home yet. All around, families plan their attacks on rows of berries, one of the earliest treats of the farmgating season.

There's something satisfying about uncovering a ripe red berry in the deep green leaves. From mid-June to mid-July, you'll see bobbing heads and swinging pails in the Saanich fields—plus many an adult with hand to aching back. One Saanich favourite is PEDERSEN BERRY FARM (6330 Central Saanich Road, off Tanner Road; 250-652-3653; daily in strawberry season; phone ahead for availability and pre-orders of picked berries).

Arnie Pedersen started this eight-hectare farm back in 1950; he was succeeded by his son, Eric, and Eric by his son, Tim. More than a hectare of Puget Reliant and Totem berries are planted out each year. Puget Reliant, in particular, is a big berry that seems to do well at Pedersen's, continuing to produce heavily till the end of the season.

Pedersen's also produces raspberries and loganberries; frozen berries are available until they are sold out.

TIM PEDERSEN'S HINTS FOR STRAWBERRY PICKERS
"A lot of people don't like the smaller berries—but a lot of smaller ones taste better than the big ones, so don't ignore them. Make sure the berries you pick are all red. In some varieties, it doesn't matter if you have a bit of white at the tip, but others won't taste right. It gets hot out there, so remember hats and sun screen. A lot of people find that one-gallon ice-cream buckets are the best for picking."

Along the Way: Oldfield Road

There's no other road like Oldfield anywhere on the island. In just a few kilometres, between Brookleigh Road and Keating Cross Road, you can find garlic and honey, chickens and strawberries, pumpkins and pies, blueberries and carrots and lettuce and apples and hothouse cucumbers and field tomatoes. The dozen or more farm stands and markets that border Oldfield and its side roads are like having a widespread farmers' market available every day of the week.

LE COTEAU FARMS is a tradition on the Peninsula. Jacques and Marianne Ponchet came to the island in the 1950s and worked on a farm. They bought the Le Coteau property on Walton Place in

Signs at Le Coteau Market, on Oldfield Road, indicate what's in season this week.

1956, growing strawberries, loganberries and raspberries they shipped to a growers' co-op and to a winery. Then they started their garden centre, selling some produce from that centre. A few years ago, their son, Dan, opened a farm market on Oldfield Road where, every year, something new gets added; the latest novelty is a U-pick flower garden. You'll find berries and vegetables from their own farm, plus a variety of produce from other farms. In the fall, check out the large number of apple and pear varieties available at the farm market. Phone for U-pick times for strawberries and blueberries. (Le Coteau market, corner of Oldfield and Bear Hill; Le Coteau farm, 304 Walton Place, 250-658-5888; *www.lecoteau.com*; 9:30 a.m. to 5 p.m. every day except Christmas and New Year's.)

In late October, Le Coteau hosts a Pumpkin Fest, with mazes, trails, a haunted house, pony rides, entertainers and other features. Check their Website for details.

On the way to Le Coteau's garden centre is BABE'S HONEY FARM (334 Walton Place, 250-658-8319; weekdays 9:30 a.m. to 4:30 p.m., Sundays 11 a.m. to 4:30 p.m.). Babe Warren sent a scare through Victoria's honey buyers and traditionalists when she told a reporter a year or two ago that she was thinking of retiring. What would Babe's Honey be without Babe, who turned 80 in 1998 and has been in the honey business since 1944?

But not to worry: Babe's family has every intention of keeping on with the business if Babe does decide to retire. You can find a variety of types of honey from both the island and other regions of BC, plus products such as beeswax and honeycomb cappings.

BLUEBEARY HILL FARM (5927 Oldfield Road, 250-652-0641) is a U-pick-only blueberry farm. Call after July 10 for the schedule or check the message board on the farmgate during blueberry season.

SUN WING GREENHOUSES (6070 Oldfield Road, 250-652-5732; daily 9 a.m. to 5 p.m., March to end of October) have expanded over the years. One of the few greenhouse producers on the Saanich Peninsula, they grow a wide variety of vine-ripened regular and cherry tomatoes, long English and white spine cucumbers, lettuces, beans and other greens, and fragrant coriander. Other non-greenhouse vegetables are available in season.

PHIL'S FARM (6080 Oldfield Road, 250-652-2264; daily to about 4 p.m. in berry season if it's not raining) is best known for its pastured poultry, raised outdoors with no antibiotics or hormones, and for its custom juicing of other people's apples. Phil feeds leftover apple pulp to his pigs; no need, he claims, for apple sauce with these pork chops, since it's already been applied internally. Raspberries and blueberries are available in season. Phone ahead for U-pick times and to order poultry and pork.

BEAR HILL RASPBERRY FARM (5939 Bear Hill Road, 250-652-1338) is hidden away along a pretty back lane flanked by signs for the Back 4-T Ranch and U-pick raspberries. Phone ahead for orders and U-pick times for raspberries, blueberries and loganberries.

At 2100 Bear Hill Road, MISTY HOLLOW FARM has a farm stand with organic vegetables.

It's been more than 15 years since Derek Scott decided that a career in the coast guard kept him away from his young family far too much. But he wasn't interested in a desk job; instead, he and wife, Debbie, decided to be farmers on an Oldfield Road property across from where she grew up.

The Scotts' OLDFIELD ORCHARD (6286 Oldfield Road, 250-652-1579; daily 9:30 a.m. to 4:30 p.m.) is now one of the busiest agritourism sites on the island. A year-round market sells pies and cinnamon buns, as well as produce the Scotts grow plus a selection from other peninsula and mainland farms and orchards. You can do a farm tour, go to Oktoberfest, attend Medieval Nights or just visit the lambs and goats and pigs that gambol and grunt for the kids. Phone or check the Website at *www.oldfieldorchard.com* for social event details.

The Scotts grow berries, apples, pears, peaches and plums on their own 10 hectares and another 15 that they lease. In season, they send a runner to the Okanagan to collect fruit picked specifically for the Oldfield Orchard stand.

Across the road is STEWART'S BERRY PATCH (6283 Oldfield Road, 250-652-6768; daily in strawberry season), another

Oldfield Orchard's Debbie Scott displays one of the market's fruit pies.

family-run farm with picked and U-pick strawberries available in season. The roadside stand at FIELDSTONE FARM (6325 Oldfield Road, 250-652-1968; daily July to November) displays some of the 10 varieties of garlic the Maxwell family grows, from strong Spanish rojo to very roastable elephant garlic. Check out BRAMBLE-SIDE FARM (1900 Nicolas Road, 250-652-4624) for tomatoes, vegetables and blackberries.

There's often a bit of a traffic jam at SKYLARK FARM (6435 Oldfield Road, 250-652-2271; daily in strawberry and raspberry season) in early summer, when strawberries and raspberries are ready: U-pickers parking in the field and lazier fruit fanciers pulling in to the stand where the berries are sold by the friendly, cheerful farm owners. Phone for U-pick times or orders.

Other stands along Oldfield Road between Bear Hill and Keating Cross Road offer produce at various times of the year. Plums, eggs, squash, rhubarb: you'll find a variety at these small stands.

Berry Good

Once upon a time, berry lovers were limited to strawberries for a few brief weeks in late June and July, followed by raspberries, followed by blackberries you picked yourself from tangled mats of berry bushes all across the peninsula. No longer. Now you need more than a dictionary or plant book to sort out the many berry types grown on the island.

- STRAWBERRIES: of course, but now you'll find everbearing and day-neutrals extending the season into mid-September.
- RASPBERRIES: still pretty traditional.
- BLACKBERRIES: thornless and many other new varieties, most of them sweeter and larger than the wild ones. Good for cooking, eating, winemaking.
- LOGANBERRIES: cross between wild blackberry and red raspberry; tart and good for wine.
- MARIONBERRY: bright, shiny, reddish-black blackberry cross developed especially for the west coast.
- TAYBERRIES: loganberry/raspberry cross.
- BOYSENBERRIES: very large loganberry/blackberry/raspberry cross, named for hybridizer Rudolph Boysen.
- BLUEBERRIES: collected wild for thousands of years in North America; domesticated in the twentieth century. Canada produces about a third of the world's blueberries. Berry growers are more and more entranced by the way they stand up to shipping and the fact they stay fresh far longer than softer berries.
- JOSTA-BERRIES: a hybrid of black currants and gooseberries.
- GOOSEBERRIES: a translucent pale green berry used more for jams and cooking than for eating raw.

GOOSEBERRY FOOLS

To play gooseberry means to be an unwanted third person, usually in the company of lovers—or to be with lovers for appearance's sake. Some say that phrase derives from the use of the word gooseberry as one of the names for the Devil—though why that was so is more than any farmgater needs to know. To play gooseberry doesn't make you a gooseberry fool: that's a pudding made with pounded gooseberries and cream. The name gooseberry probably has more to do with "gorse" than "goose."

Silver Rill Corn

Wendy Fox has been up since 4:30 a.m., but she still has the energy at mid-afternoon to discuss her golden retriever, Casey, with a fan of the breed. This Saturday before Labour Day is the busiest day of the year at SILVER RILL CORN (7117 Central Saanich Road, 250-652-3854; daily). Thousands of cobs of Peaches and Cream, super-sweet and crunchy-sweet corn will be plucked from the bins between 7 a.m., when the first customers arrive—often on their

Customers check out the corn and other produce at Silver Rill.

way home from delivering someone to the airport or the ferry and eager to load up at the best-known corn supplier on the peninsula—and midnight, when the last customer slips his money into the honour box at the stand.

Ken Fox has been growing corn on the Saanich Peninsula for almost 40 years. His wife, Wendy, and their children, Clayton and

HOW TO BUY AND COOK CORN

The fresher the corn, the better the taste. That's why hundreds of people trek to Saanich Peninsula farms from August through September, looking for corn just brought in from the fields.

You don't need to strip the husk down to check for good corn (and if you refrain, the farmers will thank you: a semi-nude cob will not be bought by anyone else if you throw it back). Go to a farm you trust—supermarket corn is considerably less likely to have been picked that day—and choose cobs that feel full all the way down.

Silver Rill and other sellers provide bins for husks if you just can't bear to take your corn home in the husk—but they do so with a sigh. Once you strip off the leaves and silk, the corn begins to deteriorate. Buy it, keep it in the refrigerator if you're not going to cook it right away (but not for more than three days) and husk it just before you pop it into boiling water. With 40 to 50 per cent sugar content, the super-sweet hybrids keep better than the older varieties.

How long to cook it? Wendy Fox says she gets supper ready, brings the corn water to the boil and slips the corn in, puts supper on the plates and takes the corn out—that's about two or three minutes in measured time. Modern corn varieties, with their smaller kernels and sweeter taste, need less cooking than corn of old. You can cook it on the barbecue or in the oven, but Wendy says boiled is best, and certainly simplest. Some butter, some salt, some pepper... and you're set.

Corrine, make this a family business. It's hard to say how Silver Rill got its reputation as *the* place to come for corn. It isn't price: when in-town supermarkets are selling corn at 10 cobs for a dollar, you have to value flavour and quality to come to Silver Rill, where 10 cobs will cost you closer to four dollars. And other farms sell the same— or similar—varieties. But there's something about Silver Rill, just off the highway, with its huge bins of corn picked the same day, a constant buzz of cars coming and going and the ever-cheerful staff, that makes it the corn stand of choice for many Victorians.

Silver Rill also sells other vegetables and fruits in season.

IT'S CORNY

What is it when you throw away the outside and eat the inside, but eat the outside and throw away the inside?

Along the Way: Brentwood

Follow West Saanich Road from Royal Oak through Brentwood and make detours on various side roads to take in a variety of farm stands and markets. In the Prospect Lake area, follow Prospect Lake Road, then Meadowbrook Road along its winding, narrow length to find MEADOWBROOK FARM (205 Meadowbrook Road, 250-479-7166; daily 9 a.m. to 9 p.m. in blueberry season) hidden away in the woods. The Yager family sells rhubarb in season, and, year-round, pepperoni made from their own beef, Mennonite sausage made from up-island pork, blueberry juice and organic beef. Phone for U-pick times and to order meat and meat products.

Several farm stands along Wallace Drive west of West Saanich Road offer a variety of products. At 5779 Wallace Drive, figs and garlic are available in season. Says the owner of this small farm: "the land decided what we would grow—garlic on the dry land higher up, figs further down." SPRING VALLEY FARM (5940 Wallace Drive) supplies produce such as beets, carrots, beans, garlic and flowers. Other stands are more anonymous, filled with produce or empty, depending the season and the garden overflow.

This country road leads to the blueberry fields of hidden-away Meadowbrook Farm.

Old West Saanich Road between West Saanich and Sparton Road also has a varying number of farm stands in operation. SPRING CREST FARM (6090 Old West Saanich Road) is reliable, but others come and go, offering plums, fresh bread, zucchini—whatever the season supplies.

VICTORIA ESTATE WINERY (14454 Benvenuto, corner Keating Cross Road, 250-652-2671) is bidding to be the largest winery on Vancouver Island, strategically placed on the route to Butchart Gardens. Designed to produce 20,000 cases of wine a year, the big

IT'S A FIGGY WEEK

As befits the fruit most mentioned in the Bible, the first week in November is National Fig Week in the United States. This puts figs one up on notaries (Nov. 7 is National Notary Public Day), funeral words (Nov. 2: Plan Your Epitaph Day) and sandwiches (Nov. 3), on a level with split pea soup in the following week, but far behind pecans (November is National Georgia Pecan Month).

winery building opens early in 2003. It is producing wines (Madeleine Sylvaner, Pinot Gris, Riesling, Chardonnay and Merlot) from Cowichan and Okanagan valley grapes. Plans call for production of wines from Saanich-grown grapes as they become available. Call for tasting and tour times.

SLUGGETT FARMS (6881 West Saanich Road, 250-385-8688 or 250-652-6396; daily 10 a.m. to 6 p.m., in season) has been in operation since John Sluggett bought 280 hectares in 1876. The nearby Baptist church is named for this deeply religious man who was also a strong advocate of temperance. At his death, he owned some 440 hectares, including two-thirds of present-day Brentwood east to East Saanich Road. The present Sluggett generation is the fourth generation to run the farm and there's a fifth almost ready to take over. The farm stand is open from June, when the first strawberries ripen, to mid-October, when the last corn is on the stand.

One of the best-looking signs en route is at RED CEDAR MOON (7513 West Saanich Road, 250-652-2088; Thursday to Saturday 8 a.m. to 6 p.m., winter 9:30 to 4:30, Sunday 9 a.m. to 1 p.m.). You'll find strawberries, raspberries, tomatoes, squash, eggs, other

At Red Cedar Moon, on West Saanich Road.

produce and preserves in the porch of this house north of Stelly's Cross Road. Chickens and turkeys can be ordered, as can quail eggs. Kiwi fruit is available in winter.

Along the Way: Central Saanich

Veyaness Road leads north off Keating Cross Road, from the industrial area into more farm fields. Look for GOBIND FARMS (6929 Veyaness, 250-652-0182, phone for times) in strawberry season: Gobind specializes in strawberries, picked and U-pick, cascade berries (another blackberry cross), boysenberries, blackberries and raspberries, as well as other seasonal produce from rhubarb to romaine lettuce. Across the road at 6922 Veyaness, look for a farm stand with tomatoes and corn for sale.

Mar's Pumpkin Patch

Lily Mar won't sit down to have her picture taken at the family's farm stand. "I'm working," she proclaims. "I don't sit down when I'm working." The always-cheerful, always-energetic Lily is a big attraction for the customers who frequent this Veyaness Road stand. Although her brothers tell her to slow down, to work less, she's not interested: she'd be out in the field harvesting if she weren't here at the stand.

MAR'S PUMPKIN PATCH (7120 Veyaness Road, 250-652-8449; daily 9 a.m. to 5:30 p.m., June to November; closed Sundays after strawberry season) is another of the Saanich Peninsula's thriving family farms. Jack Mar has been a full-time farmer on the peninsula all his adult life. Though this stand is called the pumpkin

Lily Mar proffers vegetables at her family farm stand.

patch, it offers far more than pumpkins: strawberries through squash, leeks and other produce, all grown on the 14 hectares the family farms. One of their specialties is Nantes carrots, sweet, crisp and excellent raw.

They stress crop rotation and crop monitoring—and, eager to avoid chemical sprays, suggest that "a few bugs or chew marks on your veggies won't hurt you."

THE REAL PUMPKIN

Want to make pumpkin pie, pumpkin soup or any other dish from scratch, rather than from the can? Choose a small pumpkin, preferably from a sweet variety grown for cooking. Cut it in half, scrape out the seeds (keeping them for drying), cut the pumpkin in pieces, and cook it as you would cook squash: steamed, boiled or baked. Roasted pumpkin seeds are tasty: there are many ways of preparing them, but the simplest is to dry the seeds for an hour in a very slow oven, toss them with oil and salt, then roast at about 150°C (300°F) for 10 to 15 minutes.

Saanichton Christmas Tree and Ostrich Farm

Joan Fleming is still a little bemused at the presence of these long-necked, heavy-bodied birds that can live to the age of 75, cruise at 50 kilometres an hour for half an hour and weigh up to 170 kilograms. But she has no regrets: she's fascinated now by ostriches and their many uses.

Fleming was perplexed 10 years ago when her brother Mike thrust an article about ostriches in front of her and told her to read it. She wanted nothing to do with raising animals (it's hard to call something this big that can't fly a bird) that cost $80,000 for a breeding pair and were known to kick harder than a soccer player and peck worse than a flock of super-sized chickens.

But she was somehow persuaded, and the Flemings bought their

EIGHT THINGS TO DO WITH OSTRICHES

EAT THEM: Ostrich meat is high-protein, low-fat. Try steaks, medallions, roasts, cutlets, sausages fresh and dried, burgers and liver pâté. Joan's favourite way of preparing ostrich meat is to pan-fry steaks in a little olive oil to medium or medium-rare. Meanwhile, prepare a packaged peppercorn sauce. Take the steak out and keep it warm; add the sauce to the pan to deglaze it. Get that bubbling, add the steak back in, heat, and serve. Oh, and ostrich meat doesn't taste like chicken.

EAT THEIR EGGS: Invite the gang before you start making the omelette: one ostrich egg is equivalent to two dozen hen's eggs. If you're making devilled egg, plan ahead. It takes 90 minutes to hard-boil an ostrich egg.

DECORATE THEIR EGGS: Make Christmas decorations, Fabergé-like eggs, hinged boxes.

MAKE A WALLET, OR A PURSE, OR A FOOTSTOOL: Ostrich leather is expensive and is prized for its strength and for the polka dots where the feather follicles were attached. A yearling ostrich produces 1.5 square metres of leather worth $600.

GO GARDENING: Use their ground-up bones for bone meal.

GET SMOOTH: Ostrich oil, from a layer of fat that is separate from the meat, is used as a skin moisturizer.

GO DUSTING: Ostrich feathers are much sought-after for feather dusters. They hold the dust, rather than spreading it around, are good for dusting computers or stereos, last forever and can be washed in warm soapy water.

LOOK FANCY: Use the feathers in your town crier's or other fancy hat. Or your feather boa.

first ostriches in 1992. Now they have a flock of about 200 ostriches; they keep some for breeding, sell some to other breeders and use others for meat, hides and a multitude of ostrich products. Ostriches are, with Christmas trees, the main product at the Saanichton Christmas Tree and Ostrich Farm (8231 East Saanich Road; 250-652-3345; *www.ostrichfarm.ca*).

There's a farm stand here, with local products and some imports from the Okanagan. Joan also specializes in growing many dahlia varieties, and sells tubers and cut flowers.

The farm offers tours and local high school students are fascinated by the ostriches, leaving with decorated ostrich eggs, ostrich pepperoni sticks or other ostrich products.

An ostrich peers at intruders in its territory.

 Along the Way: Saanichton

WINDY HILL FARM (7170 Maber Road, corner of Stelly's Cross Road; 250-652-2777) specializes in berries—strawberries, raspberries, tayberries, boysenberries, loganberries, blackberries—and also has some produce on its farm stand. Phone to check U-pick times. Closed Sundays.

The season at MT. NEWTON BLUEBERRIES (1450 Mt. Newton Cross Road, 250-652-6154; daily) extends into September for U-pick and picked blueberries.

Nearby is RAVENHILL HERB FARM (1330 Mt. Newton Cross Road, 250-652-4024) where cook and cookbook author Noël Richardson and gardener Andrew Yeoman offer fresh-cut herbs and herb plants, April through July, Sundays only, noon to 5 p.m.

You can bring a lunch to ROSEMEADE FARMS (1939 Meadowbank,

off Seabrook, off Stelly's Cross, 250-652-1862) and punctuate your picking by taking a break on the lawn. Rosemeade has U-pick and picked strawberries, raspberries and cascade berries, as well as beans, apples, sour cherries, rhubarb, plums, kale and corn.

You should definitely phone ahead to MEADOW BROOK MANOR (1490 Hovey Road, 250-652-5227), a specialty farm tucked away on a truly rural lane, horses on one side, fields on both. But it's worth it: Meadow Brook is the only place on the island where you'll find josta-berries, and one of the few that grow black, white and red currants as well as gooseberries. Pamela and Richard Engqvist took Pamela's father's advice: a long-time farmer who hated the cows he raised, he recommended they find something unique to grow. They decided on currants and other small fruits. A hybrid between black currants and gooseberries, josta-berries aren't as strong-tasting as currants or as sour as gooseberries. Like currants and gooseberries, they make good pies, jams and concentrates. They're available fresh in July, frozen year-round. Pamela sells jams, jellies, concentrates and other products at the Saanich Peninsula market.

NOT BERRY PICKY

Love the flavour of currants and gooseberries, but definitely not in love with the picky process of cleaning them? Pamela Engqvist says life gets much easier if you freeze the berries first, from the field to the freezer in plastic bags. When you want them, take out a cup at a time, put it in a plastic bag and roll it around between your hands, then on the counter. Put the berries into the insert of a salad spinner (or a heavy strainer) and shake them around. Then pull out all the strigs (the stems the berries grow on), rinse them off, and they're ready for use. These berries will last almost forever in the freezer with very little loss of taste.

Hillside Farm

Today's scarecrow is a giant chicken, huge yellow feet splayed out from his blue jeans, arm cradled around a mop-and-pail stringed instrument. He's an indication that life isn't altogether serious at Joanne and Tad Stoch's HILLSIDE FARM (1748 Mt. Newton Cross Road, 250-652-0650; *www.hillsidefarm.ca*; Wednesday and Saturday 9 a.m. to 6 p.m.). The next indication is Joanne herself, whose runaway enthusiasm for all things agricultural is contagious. And then there's Tad, who falls into a natural, straw-chewing farmer's pose beside the chicken.

Hillside Farm's entrepreneurial chicken welcomes visitors to the farm stand.

Beyond their obvious love of their farm, which produces eggs, raspberries, rhubarb, beans, lettuce and a dozen other produce items that are displayed on the farm stand, the Stochs' desire to make a lifestyle of their small farm is clear. Joanne stresses farm tours for younger children, introducing them to the barnyard animals—chickens, geese, ducks, turkeys, rabbits, goats, a horse—and letting them know that the things they eat don't begin life in the supermarket. A graphic artist by training and trade, Joanne also offers Art on the Farm, outdoor art activities for children 11 and up.

Now at the farm stand, Joanne is involved in a long conversation with a customer who wants a pound or two of pole beans. Not available yet, early on a Saturday morning. But that's no problem: Tad is dispatched to the garden to pick the beans. The chicken would expect no less.

Peninsula Country Market

There's something of the country fair about the PENINSULA COUNTRY MARKET, held on Saturday mornings at the Saanich fairgrounds on Stelly's Cross Road west of Wallace Drive (91528 Stelly's Cross). Entertainers sing folk songs to the accompaniment of lutes and fiddles, the smell of coffee and cinnamon is on the air and any number of people make a weekly journey to buy produce, flowers, honey, baked goods, whatever is available this week, and to sit in the sunshine and listen to the music.

Many of the larger farm producers on the peninsula have stands here each week. There's also a community stand, where various producers consign produce and other farm goods. The market is one of the largest and busiest on the island.

Along the Way: North Saanich

Trucks block the gate and workmen are setting up a huge tent on a September Saturday at the CHALET ESTATE WINERY (11195 Chalet Road, Deep Cove, 250-656-2552; Tuesday to Sunday 11 a.m. to 5 p.m. in summer, Thursday to Saturday 1 to 5 p.m., Sunday 1 to 4 p.m. off-season). The first producing winery on the Saanich Peninsula, Chalet hosts scheduled special events and group tours year-round as well as offering individual tastings.

The winery produced its first wine from Okanagan grapes in 2000, from island grapes in 2001. It has a tasting room and a small art gallery—where the works of local artists are displayed—as well as tables set out alongside the vines for large tours and tastings.

At the Saanich Peninsula country market.

Co-owner Linda Plimley notes that the climate here in North Saanich is very similar to that in the Cowichan Valley. Chalet produces wines from grapes grown on its own 1.2 hectares and on four hectares grown under contract by other farmers, as well as from non-island grapes.

HAZELMERE FARMS (11368 West Saanich Road, 250-655-8887) has been a fixture in the Deep Cove area for more than a decade. Their market building and/or roadside stand features a wide range of gourmet lettuces and other salad vegetables, Asian vegetables, basil, beets, potatoes, flowers, strawberries and other fruit and produce.

Glamorgan Road winds along the edge of Sandown Race Track off McDonald Park Road. Look here for the character buildings of Glamorgan Farm, established in 1871, and two roadside stands: one sells surplus produce from the North Saanich Allotment Gardens; the other, a variety of produce from Glamorgan farm.

GLENEDEN FARM (Landsend Road, 250-656-1688) specializes in marionberries; they also have loganberries and apples. Phone ahead for orders.

 ## The Smyths

Lorraine Smyth tucks extra beans and a pattipan squash into my parcel of produce. When I say how well basil goes with these, she insists I take a stalk or two of that fragrant herb along as well. It's clear it's a labour of love, this one-hectare garden on West Saanich Road (corner, Downey and West Saanich Road) near the north end of the peninsula, where Lorraine and husband Don grow whatever strikes their fancy.

They started out with loganberries, but now their sign on the road lists a dozen or more products from beans to berries, some of the 60 fruits and vegetables they grow. In the garden, beans grow up poles or bush out between rows of kale and huge tomato plants. Closer to the road, a vast variety of apple trees are espaliered along wires and poles.

Lush gardens at the Smyths.

The Smyths bought the property (once part of a hop farm) in 1978, when it was a hayfield, because they wanted enough land for their kids to run around. "We just got upset one day about cutting the lawns," smiles Lorraine, "so we started plotting." Before they knew it, they had a garden big enough for them to sell produce to passersby.

Now they are experimenting with cordon apples, the trees grown on an angle on metal rods, and cordon-trained figs. And they'll keep on trying new crops, as long as they are having fun.

metchosin–sooke

I'M DRIVING ONE OF MY FAVOURITE Metchosin back roads when I see a farm sign pointing down towards the water. A stand with corn and garlic and honey and leeks is there, at the end of a short side road—and so is an invitation to follow a path across a farm field (shut the gate after you, please) to a sunny overlook atop the cliff. And I think, how like Metchosin to assume the passerby has time to go for a stroll and to provide the path to do so. For this rural area west of Victoria and its neighbour, Sooke, are definitely about enjoying the countryside and definitely not about speed.

At the Metchosin market.

Walter Colquohon Grant was the first independent English settler on Vancouver Island, bucking the Hudson's Bay Company's monopoly in the mid-nineteenth century. Keeping the best farming lands for themselves, the company men sent him west along the coast, suggesting he might take up land in Metchosin. He improved on that suggestion by continuing on to the then-isolated area of Sooke. Though he did his best, clearing land and raising cattle and chickens, his best wasn't very good—he had the opposite of the Midas touch—and he's probably remembered most for introducing Scotch broom to the island, an innovation that has him heartily cursed by those who prefer native vegetation to that vigorous invader.

Grant's discovery that it was difficult to wrest a living from the stony ground west of Victoria has been born out in the succeeding decades. Though there are pastures where lambs gambol in the spring, vegetable patches and berry and fruit farms, few people support themselves by farming in Metchosin or Sooke. But many have hobby farms or farm as one of several businesses. You'd be hard pressed to collect your basket of farm produce by simply wandering from stand to stand in the region—but going to the markets on Saturday or Sunday or phoning ahead to the various producers during the week should let you gather all the bounty you want. Be forewarned, though:

66

"*Well adapted for sheep, of which there are a fair number produced; the presence of panthers, however, in the outlying district is detrimental to the profitable production in large numbers. . . .*

Were I asked where to locate a poultry farm in the province, I should unhesitatingly recommend this district. The comparatively easy work in connection with this industry, the proximity to markets, the climate, the good prices obtainable at all seasons of the year for fowls and eggs, all point to poultry raising as the one branch of agricultural pursuits for which this district is best adapted."

—REPORT OF THE BRITISH COLUMBIA
DEPARTMENT OF AGRICULTURE, 1902

even if you think you have just half an hour to spend at your farm-gating task, you may discover you have whiled away half the day, chatting, chomping, wandering and admiring the view.

The Markets

- METCHOSIN FARMERS' MARKET, Sundays 11 a.m. to 2 p.m., May through October, Happy Valley Road just west of Metchosin/William Head Road.
- SOOKE COUNTRY MARKET, Saturdays 10 a.m. to 2 p.m., mid-May through September (includes crafts as well as farm products), 2047 Otter Point Road (inland from the traffic light in Sooke).

The Route

Though there aren't a lot of roadside stands in the area, you should find some stands along Metchosin and William Head roads in Metchosin. It's always pleasant to follow Ocean Boulevard past Fort Rodd Hill and Esquimalt Lagoon. Follow Lagoon Road to Metchosin Road, turn left on Metchosin to follow it to William Head, then continue on Rocky Point, East Sooke and Gillespie roads to Sooke Road and on to Sooke. Check out stands on Kemp Lake and Otter Point roads beyond Sooke.

The Metchosin Market

It's 11 a.m. on a Sunday morning and there's a Metchosin traffic jam in the market parking lot: three cars seeking spaces on the grass beyond the market stalls. Those who frequent this market know the rules: if you don't get here early, the best stuff will be gone. Sure, there will still be produce available and John will have more sausages on the grill—but Joan will probably have sold her last strawberries, the best tomatoes will have gone into the basket of the person in front of you and there won't be a loaf of bread in view.

Metchosin's market earns merit points for its easy-going nature: vendors who all know one another joking about this product or that and sending you to someone else if they don't have what you

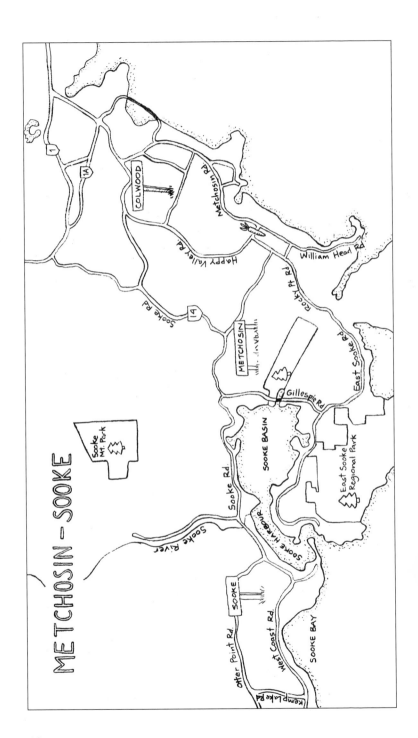

Strawberries are a feature at the Metchosin market.

want, regular customers with regular routines, a general sense of relaxation in the sunshine.

It's probably the best place to get Metchosin-area produce. Since many of the farmers in the area are part-timers—and because there have been problems with passersby taking money from unattended farm stands—many producers in the western communities bring their best produce to market for a once-a-week selling spree.

It's also one of the best places to visit to collect good things to eat for your Sunday hike to a nearby beach. That is, of course, if you have been able to resist the on-site Galloping Goose Sausages, dripping with sauerkraut and mustard....

Along the Way: Metchosin

John Harris (BLUE HAZE FARM, 3817 Duke Road, 250-474-5043) likes to experiment: he grows a variety of apples and pears but also figs, quince and crabapples. Check out his housefront stand from August through October.

Farther west, SEA BLUFF FARM (542 Wootton, off Metchosin Road near Happy Valley) provides one of those happy side treats for farmgaters. Current owner Bob Mitchell's father turned over some of this farm for the enjoyment of Metchosin residents, but they won't mind if strangers enjoy the walkway too. Follow Wootton to its end and park to check out the farm stand: corn, pumpkins, squash, leeks, honey and wool duvets are available. You can then follow the pathway (close all gates after you pass through) to the top of the cliff overlooking Juan de Fuca Strait, stop a while at a picnic table, then continue through the woods in a rectangular tour back to your car.

HAPPY VALLEY LAVENDER AND HERB FARM (3505 Happy Valley Road, 250-474-5767) focusses more on lavender than on other products. It is well worth a visit on the mid-July weekends when the lavender harvest is in process. Call for precise times. Peter Tasker sells honey and apples at QUAILS' ROOST FARM (4129 Happy Valley Road, 250-478-1329; phone ahead). EISENHAWER ORGANIC PRODUCE (4266 Happy Valley Road, 250-474-7161; phone ahead) sells mainly at markets in Metchosin and Victoria, but also offers some 30 vegetable varieties at the farm. SWALLOW HILL FARM (4910 William Head Road, 250-474-4042; phone ahead) commands a spectacular view out over farm fields and the

Visitors can wander from the Sea Bluff Farm stand along a path to a cliff overlooking the seafront.

distant water. Peter and Gini Walsh sell apples, rhubarb, yellow plums, garlic, flowers, blueberries, eggs and Asian pears, a cross between apples and pears. And if you really like the view, you can stay at their bed and breakfast.

THE WHIMSICAL FRUIT

It can be hard to love a quince—unless you cook it first. Its official name, *Cydonia oblonga*, derives from the name of an ancient Greek town: quinces have been around for a long time. They are used in jellies and jams, preserves and distillations but hardly ever raw. Its raw taste has been politely described as "astringent." Its hard, creamy yellow-white flesh turns red when cooked, while its taste is variously referred to as "indescribable" and with "the whimsical tropical quality of guava."

A drive along William Head and Rocky Point roads sometimes reveals roadside stands with produce set out by local gardeners, farmers and bakers. GALLOPING GOOSE sausages produced by Metchosin sausage-maker John Wessels, on sale cooked on market day, are available in the freezer at the Metchosin General Store at the corner of Metchosin and Happy Valley roads.

Shady Lane Farm

Joan Mendum heads her small tractor for the Mendums' century-old farmhouse, towing behind her a small wagonload of plump red strawberries, freshly picked for a Sooke gourmet restaurant. I taste one, and am in no doubt about why these strawberries are among the first products to sell out at the weekly Metchosin market. Available well into September, they have the flavour of sunny July.

Joan and Clifford Mendum run SHADY LANE FARM (4588 William Head Road, 250-478-0252; call ahead) on five hectares here and down the road. Subtly coloured bunches of flowering statice stand in buckets along the fence, ready for market. The squash patch is full and a helper is picking the marionberries that grow thick and shiny black along the vines. In the jam kitchen, jars of loganberry and bumbleberry jam are lined up, ready for sale.

Joan treasures the farming heritage of Metchosin and is a frequent spokesperson for area farmers. She keeps a Devonshire cream recipe used for years by the Fernie sisters, who had a teahouse nearby until their enterprise was felled by strict licensing regulations. Though she sells mostly at the Metchosin and Sidney markets, you can buy from the farmhouse as well.

 ## Along the Way: Sooke

From Metchosin, back roads and the main road wind mainly through forest on their way to Sooke. This isn't the best farmgating territory. Most of the few farms are tucked away off the main road and sell at the Saturday Sooke market or to local restaurants that have recognized the value of fresh local produce. But there is always a chance of finding farm stands open or places where you can get produce if you phone ahead. Your best chance is to turn right on Otter Point Road at the Sooke stoplight, and follow it either all the way to the West Coast Road or turn left on Kemp Lake Road halfway along. An intriguing stall at 2339 Kemp Lake Road suggests that garlic champagne and other garlic products are available in season.

Pasture land in Sooke.

THE FARM—otherwise known as the Sooke Chicken Farm (6606 Helgeson Road, off Otter Point, 250-642-0345)—is run by mother and daughter Laurie Morrell and Judy Thompson. You can get free-range poultry here, though if you want fresh, not frozen, especially Cornish hens and turkeys, you'd do better to phone ahead. Also here: turkey sausage, pepperoni, ground turkey, eggs.

Tugwell Creek Honey Farm

Robert Liptrot has partaken of the nectar of the gods—and now he wants you to try it too.

Mead, the nectar made from honey, has a long history, probably the longest of any alcoholic beverage. Aeons ago, Africans discovered that honey they looted from wild bees fermented to produce a marvellous nectar. It's said that remnants of mead have been discovered in Egyptian tombs (now there's a vintage for you); the Greek gods sipped mead and the Celts revered it.

It's a long way from Greek gods to Sooke, but Liptrot makes the leap: his bee-to-bottle farmgate meadery is the island's first, opening in 2003. Liptrot and partner Dana LeComte own TUGWELL CREEK HONEY FARM (8750 West Coast Road, 11 km west of Sooke, 250-642-1956; Wednesday to Sunday 11 a.m. to 4 p.m., April through August). They produce some 1,360 kilograms of fireweed and salal flower honey for sale each year from their hundred beehives.

Liptrot has been fascinated by bees since he was six years old and helping his neighbours with

Apiarist Robert Liptrot opens a hive.

GOING TO A MEAD-TASTING?

Some things you should know:

- TRADITIONAL MEAD: made from honey and water.
- SACK MEAD: contains 20 to 25% more water than traditional mead.
- METHEGLIN: contains honey, water and various herbs.
- SACK METHEGLIN: contains 20 to 25% more water than traditional metheglin.
- CLARRE OR PYMENT MEAD: honey and grape juice.
- CYSER: honey and apple juice.
- MULSUM OR MELOMEL: honey, water and fruit juice other than apple.
- MORAT: honey, water and mulberries.

And no, mead is not as sweet as honey; the fermentation process converts much of the sugar to alcohol.

their beehives. After a detour through an MA in entomology and a job in Vancouver, he came back to his first love in 1995, when he and LeComte established the farm where he also gives courses for beekeepers. They sell honey and packages of bees—and now mead. They plan to produce a vintage mead that some compare in taste to fine sherry, plus a less expensive beverage.

Tugwell also provides, for a fee, extended tours and beekeeping information.

HAPPY HONEYMOON

In ancient (or not so ancient) Ireland, a newlywed couple ate honey on their bridal night and every night for a month thereafter, to ensure fertility and the birth, it was hoped, of a son. Therefrom comes the word "honeymoon."

the gulf islands

FOR ME, THE GULF ISLANDS have always been a bit of a farmgate conundrum: I know that a wide variety of fascinating farm products are grown and raised on the islands, but, like access to island ocean beaches, they seem elusive. Round that corner, or the next one, I think—but somehow the farm stands evade me. Ask a local and they'll say, "Well, everyone's always at the market." Yet dig a little deeper and ask a few more questions and people start to tell you about the stands where they buy their own produce.

The Gulf Island farm landscape is characterized by sheep pastured on the rolling hills.

As anywhere else, surviving solely from a small farm operation is difficult. But the Gulf Islands are still mostly rural, people are fiercely loyal to their own and the big-box mentality is largely absent—all factors that create a closer tie to farmer-producers here than in the city.

It doesn't seem surprising that two premier cheesemakers live and work here, or that one of those cheesemakers declares that Saltspring Island might be the only place where she and her partner could have made a success of what even she describes as a "loony venture." Nor does it surprise that island farm markets are busy and successful. Islanders treat markets as a place to meet and mingle, and their liking for the eclectic means they'll line up for unusual products and produce.

Agriculture has a relatively long history in the Gulf Islands. Settlers in the mid-nineteenth century found that land was cheaper—though less promising—here than in the Cowichan or Comox valleys. The settlers were less concerned with producing for market than they were with supporting themselves from their gardens and small farms.

"

"The climate of these islands is equable in the extreme, and, consequently, well adapted for fruit culture, which industry is carried on to a considerable extent and with great success. On account, also, of their immunity from predatory animals, the raising of sheep is most successfully prosecuted. . . . Their immunity from the sea breezes that affect the southern end of Vancouver Island so much during the summer, renders them much better adapted to the less hardy varieties of fruit and vegetables such as peaches, apricots, nectarines, grapes, figs, melons, tomatoes and corn. These should be attempted to be grown in much greater degree than is now done. It is too often the case that the traditional belief that a country is only good for some things and not for others results in no attempt being made to disprove the belief. As a matter of fact, those who have made a genuine attempt to grow many of the products mentioned have succeeded beyond all expectations."

—REPORT OF THE DEPARTMENT OF AGRICULTURE, 1902

∧ Farm fields stretch west on Saanich's Martindale Flats.

∧ A farmgate stand on the Saanich Peninsula offers produce to passersby.

> Wendy and Corrine Fox at Silver Rill Farm with their dog, Casey, who gives new meaning to the term corn dog.

∧ Lorraine Smyth picks beans for the farm stand at her Saanich garden.

∧ The view at Swallow Hill Farm in Metchosin.

∧ The carefully tended gardens at Providence Farm, near Duncan.

> Cheesemaker Julia Grace with one of the Jersey cows that provides the milk for Saltspring Island's Moonstruck Cheese.

∧ Farm children cuddle up to the menagerie at Evans Acres, near Qualicum Beach.

> Blueberries at Cobble Hill's Silverside Farm.

∧ Farm fields west of Port Alberni.

∧ Pumpkins brighten the day at Acacia Acres, in the Comox Valley.

> Long English cucumbers dangle from the vines in one of the greenhouses at Sieffert's farm in the Comox Valley.

By the 1930s, there were three hectares under greenhouse glass on Mayne Island, an endeavour that Japanese Canadians excelled at until their expulsion in 1942. Island Brand tomatoes and cucumbers, packed at a co-operative packing plant, were well known, and some 50 tonnes of tomatoes were sent off-island every year.

Today's Gulf Islanders are in the forefront of the organic movement in the province and are more than willing to experiment—one farmer has even planted an olive grove on North Pender. Though the markets are the best bet for those who want to stock their larders with a wide range of island produce, wandering the back roads usually reveals impromptu or established farm stands, and small stores often carry local produce.

The Markets

- SALTSPRING ISLAND FARMERS' MARKET, Saturdays 8 a.m. to 4 p.m., April through October, Centennial Park, downtown Ganges.
- MAYNE ISLAND FARMERS' MARKET, Saturdays from 10 a.m., July through September, Agricultural Hall grounds.
- PENDER ISLAND FARMERS' MARKET, Saturday mornings, late May to October, Pender Island Community Hall, North Pender.
- SATURNA ISLAND MARKET, Saturdays 1 to 4 p.m., July and August, Community Hall.

WORTH GOING TO

The Saltspring Apple Festival takes place in late September at the Fulford Hall, Apple Luscious Orchard and various farms around Saltspring; call 250-653-2007 for details. This is one of the few days in the year when a majority of Saltspring farms welcome visitors. It's described as an "apple tasting extravaganza of the best selection, tastiest and most wholesome apples anywhere."

The Route

It's difficult to define a precise route for would-be farmgaters on the Gulf Islands: drive any of the roads in season to seek out

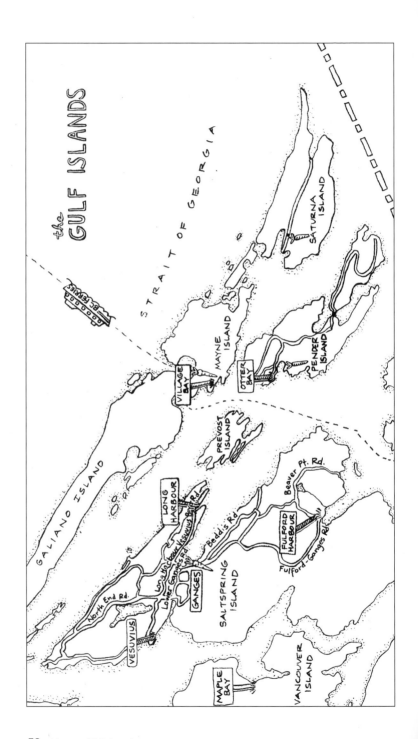

farm stands. As with most other things, SALTSPRING ISLAND has the most farm stands and farm markets, plus the biggest and best-known official farmers' market. Farm stands pop up on both PENDER ISLAND and MAYNE ISLAND and, to a lesser degree, on SATURNA ISLAND, where a winery also welcomes visitors. Galiano Island, more forest than farmland, is less likely to reward farmgaters.

Saltspring Island
Apple Luscious

Harry Burton steps off the path to pick a rosy apple—and almost disappears into the undergrowth. The trees at APPLE LUSCIOUS ORGANIC ORCHARD (110 Heidi Place, 250-653-2007; open August to October) are not part of your average neatly

groomed apple orchard. Burton believes in letting nature take over, so you have to keep your eyes open as you walk or risk stumbling into a patch of nettles or tripping over a clucking chicken or lurking cat.

Burton carries a pair of secateurs in his pocket as he walks, whipping them out to cut back the blackberries to allow us through. His delight in his wild orchard is more than evident as he plucks a mottled Wynoochie Early from a tree and passes it over, daring me to prefer a "city apple"—apples for those who care more about looks than taste. He shakes his head over scab on a variety that isn't

Harry Burton in his wild orchard.

growing well and launches into praise for a patch of thistles that are hosts for beneficial insects and good for the soil.

Burton has owned this land for some years, but he came here full time only in 1998, when he set about rehabilitating the orchard. He started a bee garden where every plant is oriented towards attracting bees, began growing Asian pears and built a light and airy coop for his chickens. And he began to live out his dream of preserving diversity in apple varieties—thus, the almost 200 varieties scattered through the orchard. He's also the mainspring behind Saltspring's Apple Festival, held every year in late September.

You can stop by the farm stand at Apple Luscious, built around huge mature maple and cedar trees and ornamented with stained glass. Phone ahead for large quantities or if you want an orchard tour.

Island Cheesemakers

David Wood likes goat cheese—it's the goats he's not so keen about.

Wood, who with wife Nancy operates SALT SPRING ISLAND CHEESE (250-653-2300), has been making sheep and goat cheese since 1996. "The good thing about sheep? They aren't goats. The only thing worse than goats is the people who keep them," he says, tongue firmly in cheek, "but it took us a long time to figure that out." Once they did, the Woods kept their flock of 100 sheep, but went to other farmers for their goat's milk.

Salt Spring Island Cheese is the pioneer island cheesemaker; their small, ripened, seasoned goat cheeses are eagerly sought after and other cheesemakers look up to the Woods and watch carefully what they do.

When they began making cheese their aim was to have a self-sufficient family life on the Saltspring farm, an aim they still find difficult to achieve. "It's finding the right balance of volume and price,"David notes. "I don't think I expected we would have to do as much volume as we do to make a living at it."

Not far away, Julia and Susan Grace tend their small herd of Jersey cows, produce organic milk and make a range of soft, semi-soft and aged white and blue cow's-milk cheeses. MOONSTRUCK

Cheesemaker David Wood with some of his cheese on Saltspring Island.

CHEESE (250-537-4987) cows are outdoor year-round and the taste of their milk changes according to what they eat—as does the taste of the cheese.

Like the Woods, the Graces are happy refugees from a faster life. "It's the best thing we ever did," notes Julia of their Moonstruck business. "We started out with a small organic market garden, but Susan was more interested in animals than plants. I was dead set against the idea of milking cows, but. . . ."

Julia is convinced that Saltspring made the difference. "The Saltspring environment supports creativity. I don't know if there is anywhere else in the country where we would have moved and started something as loony as organic cheese.

HINTS ON THE CHEESE COURSE FROM DAVID WOOD

A good cheese course has three cheeses—not more than four—to choose from. The key to a good cheese course is variety of tastes and textures. Don't include, for example, both a goat's-milk Camembert and a cow's-milk Camembert. Have a surface-ripened cheese like a blue or a Camembert and a harder cheese, like an Edam or Cheddar. Combine a goat, a cow, a sheep cheese.

Another approach is to have just one cheese with a selection of other things that go with it: goat cheese perhaps, with figs or walnuts or walnut bread; sheep cheese with quince jelly, a traditional accompaniment in Spain; blue cheese with Carr's wholemeal biscuits; or pepper goat cheese with smoked tuna.

"One thing that's wonderful about cheese—we all struggle with the amount of time we take to produce a good meal—and twenty minutes, and it's over. But put a cheese plate on the table, and people will sit and talk for an hour."

Health department regulations mean that visitors can't enter the cheesemaking facilities. Phone or check around on the Web to discover where to purchase cheeses, which are available at the Saltspring Market and at Saltspring and Victoria outlets.

WHY IS BLUE CHEESE BLUE?

Many makers of blue cheese add a tiny amount of the same type of mould that grows on your rye bread to the cheese curd—as little as a teaspoonful to 200 litres of milk—when the conditions are right for the mould to flower. It then makes its way through the cheese, giving blue cheese its characteristic acrid snap. Other cheesemakers insert needles into the cheese; mould grows in the resulting holes. The earliest blue cheeses probably occurred by accident when mould grew on cheeses stored in damp caves. The first person to sample these mouldy cheeses instead of throwing them out discovered their distinctive taste.

Along the Way: Near Fulford Harbour

Farmgating on Saltspring, as on any Gulf Island, can be hit and miss: only a few stands are open regular hours, and what you find depends very much on what matured or ripened that week. But that's part of the fun of farmgating—don't plan your dinner menu ahead of time and watch for signs along the road as gardeners put out their surplus fruit and vegetables for sale.

A farm stand between Fulford Harbour and Ganges.

At Saltspring's south end, near the ferry terminal, try STAN'S VEGE-TATION STATION, on the Fulford-Ganges Road just up from the Isabella Point Road corner. The WHITE HOUSE, across from the Fulford fire hall on the Fulford-Ganges road, offers pork, poultry, eggs, vegetables, jam, bread and apples. Farther along the road, try MANDERLAY GARDENS, where you can gaze with awe at greenhouse orchids before you buy your fresh vegetables. Across the road from Salt Spring Cheese, the STOWEL LAKE FARM stand (190 Reynolds, Tuesday and Friday noon to 7 p.m.) offers mixed veg, eggs, berries and other products. Look for several farm stands on Beddis Road, one at 765 Beddis and another at the Walter Bay Rest Stop.

The Saturday Market

Some call it a zoo, some call it the best market they've seen any-where—and both groups are right. The Saltspring market is the biggest and busiest of island markets, with people ferrying over for the produce, crafts and food laid out for sale by more than a hundred island vendors. It even has its own Website—*www.saltspringmarket.com.*

In July and August, you'll fight other off-islanders for a parking space—but that doesn't make the market any less attractive if what you are after is colour and variety. You'll find island-grown garlic, eggs, asparagus, radishes; island-made bread, cheese, pickles, preserves, stone-milled flour; smoked tuna to go with your island cheese. Tie-dye and all-natural dog biscuits are available as well: this is the place to verify that Saltspring is half-hippy and half-entrepreneur. The lone market rule is that everything for sale must be grown or made by the seller.

Among the vendors are a half-dozen certified organic farms.

 ## Along the Way: Ganges to Vesuvius

Can't make it to the market? Need something on a day other than Saturday? Check out the GROWING CIRCLE FOOD CO-OP (106-149 Fulford-Ganges Road, 250-537-4247) in the mini-mall behind the Petro-Canada station in Ganges. The produce is good and the farm names intriguing: you can buy tomatoes, beans, tiny potatoes and a raft of other fruit and vegetables from Seven Ravens, Stone Glen, Cackleberry, Whims, Lavender Hill and many other farms and growers.

Just out of the centre of Ganges is 1.2-hectare INDIGO FARM (289 Rainbow Road; year-round, until produce runs out), where

A farm stand and barn on the north end of Saltspring Island.

CAN YOU GET CARDOONS ON SATURDAY MORNING?
No, that's not a typo: look for cardoon, a type of artichoke, at the Saltspring market. Those who know cardoons advise that mice like the seeds, that only the leafstalks and top of the stalk can be eaten, that they are cranky about the way they are harvested, and that they take up so much room in the garden that they can scarcely pay for themselves as a crop.

you'll find strawberries, raspberries, carrots, many other vegetables, plus bagged salad mix, eggs and chickens to order. Not far from Ganges, look for garlic and garlic products plus smoked salmon at LEISURE LANE GARLIC (150 Leisure Lane, 250-537-1210). Check out the farm stand at 111 Leisure Lane, where a sign encourages you, "Don't see what you want? Ask and we'll pick it fresh."

Follow North End Road out past St. Mary Lake, and you'll come upon NORTHEND FARM MARKET (2521 North End Road, 250-537-4442; daily 10 a.m. to 5:30 p.m. year-round) set well back off the road. Here, you can get blueberries and strawberries well into September, plus strawberry and other fruit jam and fleeces and other wool products from farm sheep. In summer, there's a small petting zoo. The greenhouse supplies tomatoes and peppers; salad greens are available year-round. Phone to order lamb.

Watch for signs along the way that point you to sales of eggs, tuna, salmon and anything else gardeners have a surplus of that week.

Follow Vesuvius Bay Road back from the Crofton-Saltspring ferry terminal for farm stands at 691 Vesuvius Bay Road (open 8 a.m. to 8 p.m.) and other nearby locations.

Mayne Island

On Mayne Island is ARBUTUS BAY DEER FARMS (770 Beechwood Drive, 250-539-2301, *www.arbutusbay.ca*), with its farmed venison and venison products, tabbed Fenison™. Paula Buchholz began farming fallow deer in 1988. "I wanted to live with the land,"

SOME HINTS FOR COOKING FARMED VENISON
Paula Buchholz warns that venison tends to dry out faster than
other red meats. Dry cooking times need to be shorter than for
beef and venison should be basted during cooking. Loin or good
leg cuts should be cooked quickly, sealing the outside while the
inside remains rare to medium-rare. Moist cooking methods for
less tender cuts are the same as for other meats.

she recalls, "and I thought that it's nicer to live with deer than with
cattle or pigs—and my sheep that I had already were not intelligent
enough to make it interesting."

The third farmer in BC to get a fallow deer farming licence,
Buchholz sells a wide range of venison cuts plus pâtés. Phone
ahead to ensure that someone is at the farm.

The Pender Islands
A number of farms and market gardens exist on Pender; best bet is
to keep a sharp eye open for roadside stands along your route or
visit the farm market on Saturday mornings.

You'll have to wait in line for a long time to buy from the Pender
Islands' newest agricultural venture. Andrew and Sandy Butt have
planted an olive grove—Frantolio olive trees from Tuscany and
Mission and Leccino trees from California—facing southwest on
the century-old homestead at Waterlea, on North Pender. The
Butts hope that they'll be producing Canada's first organic extra
virgin olive oil by 2007.

Saturna Island
Saturna is the most hidden of the southern Gulf Islands, the least
populous and the most difficult to get to. It seems strange, then,
that Saturna is home to the Gulf Islands' only winery. And,
indeed, eyebrows were raised when the owners of Saturna Lodge
began planting grapevines in the mid-1990s. But SATURNA ISLAND

VINEYARDS AND WINERY (8 Quarry Trail, 250-539-5139 or 250-539-3521, *www.saturnavineyards.com*) has been producing wine since 1999; its wine list now includes Chardonnays, Rieslings, a Pinot Gris, Merlots and others. The wine shop is open seven days a week, 11:30 a.m. to 4:30 p.m., May through September, and Saturdays and Sundays 11:30 a.m. to 4 p.m. in October and November.

cowichan valley

IF YOU'RE WANDERING the farmgates of the Cowichan Valley or chatting with a Cowichan producer, one thing is certain: it won't be very long before you hear that the valley is Canada's Provence.

At first glance, the resemblance is tenuous. Provence is famed for sun and blue sky, the colours of the fields, the bustle of the markets. Though there's sun and blue sky enough in Cowichan, no one has yet written best-selling books about life in the valley. A second glance, though, shows why the metaphor was born. Cowichan is a gentle land, with wineries, berry fields and herb gardens scattered

Workers pick blueberries at a Cowichan Valley farm.

along the picturesque back roads. Increasingly, restaurants in the valley are experimenting with what is grown and raised in the valley, and farmers are reciprocating by experimenting with new crops. Cowichan's Feast of Fields—where area chefs prepare amazing dishes from local foods—attracts hundreds of people every year, the slogan "slow food" is increasingly recognizable, and the valley now boasts a cooking school dedicated to regional produce.

Markus Griesser, the manager of The Aerie Resort, which has a worldwide reputation, is one of the main proponents of Cowichan as Provence. You only have to see him wax eloquent over the seafood, the pasture-raised chickens, the great variety of salad greens, the unusual and the unexpected from Cowichan farms, to know that here is a man on a mission: Griesser wants the world to know what Cowichan has to offer.

He's not the first to spot Cowichan's potential. As an early correspondent noted, "This district is particularly adapted for the pursuit of both agriculture and horticulture.... The soils respond readily to cultivation and produce large crops.... Grapes grown in this district have been proved capable of producing a wine of very high quality."

"

"He [early settler Jean Campagnon] had only been here two years and yet what had formerly been a wild desert was now in such a state of cultivation that it was difficult to suppose ourselves in one of the wildest of the wild districts of Vancouver Island. He had about 100 acres under cultivation & the soil was of the very richest quality—in fact he told us it would grow anything.... Beet roots he was growing for sugar & considered the climate & soil remarkably suitable for it. He presented us with some fine Cowichan grown tobacco & considered that the whole valley might be planted with it.... To our supper, he added some trout, raddishes & onions."

—ROBERT BROWN, 1864, IN *ROBERT BROWN AND THE VANCOUVER ISLAND EXPLORING EXPEDITION* (VANCOUVER: UBC PRESS, 1989)

Though it took another century for sufficient grapes to be grown and wines to be made in commercial quantity, visiting wineries is a major highlight of farmgating in the Cowichan Valley today. Wine-tasting leads the visitor along the back roads both east and west of the Island Highway, past a number of farms and farmgate stands that offer some of the island's best raspberries and blueberries, herbs and produce, lamb and poultry.

The Markets

A vendor at the downtown Duncan farmers' market offers produce to passersby.

- NEW DUNCAN FARMERS' MARKET, Saturdays 9 a.m. to 2 p.m., Canada Avenue downtown by the train station, mid-May to December.
- COWICHAN VALLEY MARKET-PLACE, Saturdays 9 a.m. to 1 p.m., Cowichan Fair Ground, Clements and James streets, year-round (farm products, crafts, collectibles, used, etc.).

The Route

The Cowichan Valley area stretches from Cobble Hill in the south to Chemainus in the north, from the waters between the island and Saltspring in the east to the mountains in the west. The farmgating route looks at four areas within the valley.

Roads angle west and north off the highway from Mill Bay through COBBLE HILL. Follow the Shawnigan-Mill Bay Road from the highway west, cut across on Cameron-Taggart Road, then follow Cobble Hill Road back to the highway to find most of the farms mentioned in this chapter.

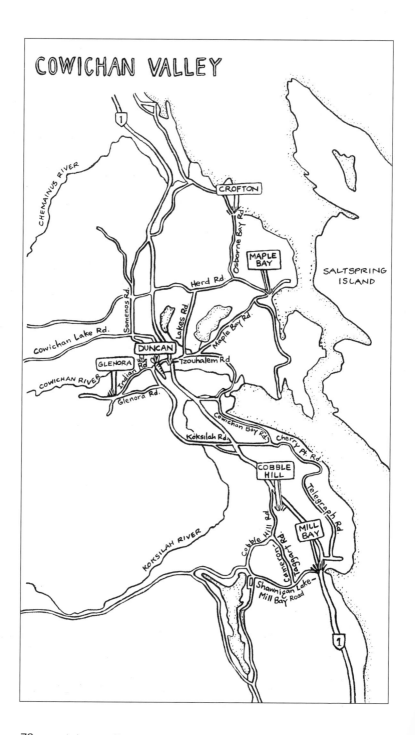

COWICHAN VALLEY

The COWICHAN BAY area runs from Mill Bay north to Duncan. Head east just north of Mill Bay on Kilmalu Road, follow Telegraph and Cherry Point roads north, then continue on Cowichan Bay Road. You can continue along the water to Tzouhalem Road, then follow back roads north towards Maple Bay and Chemainus, or head west through Duncan and beyond.

WEST OF THE HIGHWAY, a maze of roads crosses farm fields and leads to hidden wineries. Best to get a good map here: there are still people out there searching, for example, for Blue Grouse vineyards. The key roads here are Koksilah, Indian and Glenora south of Duncan, Gibbins west of town.

NORTH AND EAST OF DUNCAN, seek out Tzouhalem, Lakes, Stamps, Maple Bay and Herd roads. A map helps here, too.

Along the Way: Cobble Hill Area

Head down the Shawnigan-Mill Bay Road, west from the highway. Turn right on Wilkinson, left on Deerwood for STONEFIELD FARM (1114 Deerwood Place, 250-743-3861; Tuesday to Saturday, 10 a.m. to 5 p.m.), where you can buy chickens, pork and pork sausages, as well as order-ahead beef and lamb. Also at this farmgate stand are salad greens, pickling cukes, garlic, a variety of herbs such as sage and savoury, green beans, and vegetarian rice and soup mixes. Stonefield's poor man's soup mix, for example, contains green and yellow peas, green and red lentils, brown rice, barley and a spice pack. You'll find bread and cookie mixes and you can order seasonal breads such as lemon blueberry loaves and chocolate zucchini bread.

Drop by the DUTCH DELI AND MEAT (1220 Shawnigan-Mill Bay Road, 250-743-4648) for home-smoked sausage, bacon and ham. Case Langhout moved his butcher business here from the Victoria area years ago; he obtains his pork from area farms.

Also in the Shawnigan-Cobble Hill neighbourhood: NIGHT-INGALE ROAD STRAWBERRY FARM (1018 Nightingale Road, 250-743-3071; U-pick by appointment only; call for hours and availability). GAMBOA GREENHOUSES (1360 Fisher Road, 250-743-9013)

Silverside Farm's Jean Aten with a basket of prized raspberries.

supplies tomatoes, cucumbers, peppers and basil, March through November.

Silverside Farm

Jean and Bill Aten's raspberries and blueberries rank with the best on the island. They are so popular that regular customers e-mail in their orders months ahead of time and the casual visitor has little chance of picking up berries. But SILVERSIDE FARM (3810 Cobble Hill Road, 250-743-9149, open every day early July to the end of August) is still worth a visit, for the berry vinegars, jams and syrups they produce and sell and the pottery and paintings on display. Sit in the sunshine with an ice-cream cone and watch the pickers at work, or browse the shop and admire Jean's paintings.

HINTS FOR FREEZING BLUEBERRIES AND RASPBERRIES

Unsprayed berries don't need washing before they are frozen. Berries from Silverside and most other farms in the region fit this category: ask when you buy. Tumble the berries gently onto a cookie sheet in a single layer and put them into the freezer. This method of freezing allows soft berries like raspberries and blackberries to retain their natural shapes. When they are frozen hard, pour them into freezer bags, remove the air, tie and label. If the berries are in open paper containers, you can put the container, berries and all, into the freezer. When the berries are frozen, pour them into bags. This will take longer than freezing them on sheets. Blueberries can also be poured directly into bags and frozen.

Merridale Cider

Al Piggott started his MERRIDALE CIDERWORKS (1230 Merridale Road, 250-743-4293; daily 11 a.m. to 5:30 p.m.) some 20 years ago, choosing this location carefully and planning what was then one of just two cider orchards in North America. He was known for his crustiness and straight-talking. Ask him why he got into the cider business and his reply was a blunt "stupidity"; ask him about commercial ciders and the words "horse piss" would always figure. Piggott sold out a few years ago, but Merridale, now owned by Janet Docherty and Rick Pipes, goes on improving, still one of the few cideries in Canada.

Wander through the orchard here and you may trip over a deer looking for windfalls. Try one or two yourself, though only one of the varieties in the eight-hectare orchard is an eating apple. The rest are cider apples, such as Tremlett's Bitter, an old variety that tastes sweet to start but quickly puckers up the mouth. No Sweet Hoary Morning apples, though, more's the pity: this traditional English cider apple must be worth growing for the name alone.

Inside, you can hear about how the cider is made and sample some varieties, including traditional English-style, scrumpy, the strong, sharp cider that got its name because it was made by farm labourers who stole or "scrumped" apples, and Somerset Select dry cider, an English-style champagne cider.

Sipping cider in the sunshine at Merridale.

Along the Way: Cowichan Bay

Farmgaters get impatient round about April, anxious to get back on the road looking for fresh produce. No surprise then to see car after car bumping its way up the lane or parking on the narrow road in front of Charles and Carole Ford's ASPARAGUS FARM (1550 Robson Lane, off Cowichan Bay Road, 250-743-5073; 10 a.m. to 3 p.m., mid-April through May, weather permitting or until sold out—which can be early in the day). The Fords' is the only farm on the island to specialize in asparagus, though there are a few others that grow the tender green and white stalks. They grow mostly green asparagus, with a little white as a continuing and expensive-to-grow alternative.

GREEN AND WHITE

Asparagus is born green; it has to learn how to be white. Much beloved by European chefs, white asparagus is the same variety as green, but grown in the dark. Traditionally, sand is piled up around the individual spears as they grow; when they are of the right size, the harvester uses a special asparagus knife to cut the spear near the root. Some growers, however, grow the vegetable under opaque plastic, making sure the only light it sees is when the spears are harvested. Europeans like what they term the lighter, more delicate flavour—"like eating butter"—while others say the white variety is asparagus for those who don't like asparagus (which rather makes one wonder why it's worth the bother).

On Telegraph Road, keep an eye out for farmgate signs. ARBUTUS RIDGE FARM (3295 Telegraph Road, 250-743-7599, late May to end October; hours vary with the season) sells tomatoes, some produce—and some of the best fine-chopped salsa found anywhere. Look next door for HARD TO COME BY FARM (3311 Telegraph Road, 250-743-3327, September to January) for 10 varieties of apples. Just down the road, on the corner of LaFortune Road, a farm stand offers produce such as beans and garlic in season. Look for a sign on Telegraph Road at Pemberton pointing towards the water and advertising peppers, tomatoes and cucumbers; a pleasant drive down enjoyable back roads leads to KILIPI GREENHOUSES at 3210 Kilipi Road.

Alwin and Connie Dryland came to the island from Alberta a few years ago, but they couldn't leave their prairie roots behind. Their SASKATOON BERRY FARM (1245 Fisher Road, 250-743-1189; daily in season, 7 a.m. to sold out) is the lone island grower of saskatoon berries, a fruit that resembles dark blueberries, but that

Alwin and Connie Dryland at their saskatoon berry stand.

has a nutty taste, almost like almonds. They also grow strawberries and chokecherries. If this is prairie friendliness, we could all use some: the Drylands are exceptionally welcoming, proffering recipes and saskatoon berry advice to all comers.

THE PRAIRIE BERRY

Ask any prairie immigrant to Vancouver Island, and they'll tell you about saskatoon berries, picked in late summer from bushes that are native to the region from Manitoba to the Rockies. Prairie native people added dried saskatoons to their pemmican. The city of Saskatoon is named after the berries, *mis-sask-guah-too-min* in the native language of the area. We're less familiar with them out here and have to learn about their unique flavour—and about how to use them. If you boil them with sugar, for example, the skins will turn tough: cook them first, add sugar afterwards. Also known as serviceberry, shadbush, Indian pear or Juneberry, the saskatoon berry is part of the 3,000-species Rosaceae plant family, which also includes the apple.

Cowichan Bay Farm

Lyle Young remembers the old days on COWICHAN BAY FARM (1560 Cowichan Bay Road, 250-746-7884; daily in summer), the cook stove and the animals and the farmhouse built in 1912. "It was like going back in time," he muses—but that's not said with nostalgia. For Young and his wife, Fiona, the efforts his grandfather made to maintain a style of farming more common in 1900 than in 2000 are evidence of common sense in the face of foolish agricultural innovation.

Young's grandfather wanted a self-sustaining farm. He had no interest in the factory-style farming, with its use of chemicals and heavy mechanization, that became popular in the late 1940s. In 1986, when he died, nothing on the farm was newer than 1945; there were no plastics or bright colours, no feedlots or pesticides. "He had respect for every living thing," Lyle recalls.

Old farm implements hang on a weathered wall at Cowichan Bay Farm.

Lyle was in Africa when his grandfather died. The future of the farm was in doubt: Lyle's grandmother, "the most courageous woman I've ever met," could not continue alone. When he returned, "she gave this kid the chance to come here and pursue his dream."

With a multitude of missteps, he and Fiona did pursue the dream of a farm without the drugs, chemicals and identical products of the big farmers. Cowichan Bay Farm today is the result of their dedication to that new/old way of farming.

Along the way, the Youngs were converted to the idea of helping to preserve genetic diversity by raising rare breeds of animals that were threatened by the rush to conformity. On Cowichan Bay Farm, you'll see San Clemente Island goats, Dexter cattle, Navajo Churro sheep. You'll also find chickens, ducks and turkeys raised both for the local restaurant trade and for farmgaters. You can buy chickens and chicken products, including smoked chicken and chicken sausage; lamb and beef are available by order September and October.

The Youngs are dedicated converts to the idea of agritourism: they want people to see how their farm operates, and they want it to be a part of the community. They offer group tours of the farm; every Father's Day weekend, they host a farm Art Show where art with an agricultural theme is on display in their barn galleries (open year-round) and artisans are at work around the farm.

WHAT'S THAT CHICKEN DOING IN AN RV?

TV footage of poor, pale chickens incarcerated in tiny cages, never to see the light of day, have made many people question how the poultry they eat is raised. But what's the alternative? Let your chickens loose on the pasture, and the raccoons may eat more chicken than you do. And those who raise chickens often find that letting them roam freely does not result in good meat birds. So many poultry raisers are trying out the "pastured poultry model." At Cowichan Bay Farm, for instance, the birds are outside every day, but they're in what Lyle Young calls "chicken RVs"—large, rolling, bottomless pens that are moved every day to a new patch of pasture. Their excreta become manure for the patch they have just left, the chickens are outdoors and have new pasture every day and their meat has, says Young, "an irresistible flavour."

Engeler Farm

Mara Jernigan describes herself as a cook who became so political about food that she had to grow her own. That explains why she and husband Alfons Oberlacher are farming two hectares of land near Cobble Hill, running a cooking school on the premises and acting as ambassadors for the slow food movement.

You won't be bored at ENGELER FARM (4255 Trans Canada Highway, 250-743-4267; *www.engelerfarm.com*), which offers special events, cooking classes and farm tours by appointment. Jernigan is in perpetual motion, dealing with suppliers of such exotica as seaweed and local mushrooms, on-line and on-phone and on-FAX with other slow foodies, working with the animals on the farm, cooking in the kitchen. She talks as she makes notes on things to do, answers the phone, makes suggestions for husband and son and farm workers, prepares lunch for all of us. It's simple pasta and salad today—but alive with fresh basil and green beans and ripe tomatoes from the garden and set off by the farm's own Pinot Gris. Some 21 different kinds of salad greens are grown at Engeler, most with less familiar names, such as Freckles and Lolla Rosa. The family also raises rare breeds—Tamworth pigs, San Clemente goats and Navajo Churro sheep.

Alfons Oberlacher picks beans for lunch at Engeler Farm.

Over the years, Jernigan worked with some of Toronto's best chefs but grew tired of the rat race and retreated to Oberlacher's family farm in Austria. They moved back to Toronto, then to Vancouver, then discovered this property beside the Island Highway south of Duncan. Here, they run a cooking school year-round, focussing on visitors to the island in summer, residents the rest of the year. Slow food—as opposed to fast food—is their priority.

"Food isn't built to travel," she notes as she frenches a pile of beans and talks about how important it is to maintain agriculture in the valley and on the rest of the island. "I grew up on convenience food. I discovered good food as a chef. We should be eating seasonally, locally, if possible organically."

The Wine Route

In the 1980s, a few brave adventurers began to take seriously the idea that the Cowichan Valley's warm climate, sunshine and fertile soils might sustain some fine vineyards.

Establishing the Cowichan Valley as a wine region was no easy

La Vinoteca, the restaurant at Vigneti Zanatta, the Cowichan Valley's first winery.

task. It required jumping the hurdles government regulation placed in front of cottage wineries, waiting for the vines to mature and produce good-quality grapes, and overcoming people's scepticism ("Wines made on the island? You must be joking!"). The process took some sheer dogged determination plus optimism plus a vision of the future. But first at Vigneti Zanatta, then at Blue Grouse, then at a handful of other wineries, vintners took up the challenge. Now, valley wineries produce medal-winning wines, both white and red. One has a thriving special-event business, one a restaurant serving locally inspired food, one a picnic area. Most welcome visitors and sell wine from their own shops. For additional information, check out *www.islandwineries.ca*.

One of the newest and the southernmost winery, located on a knoll in Cobble Hill west of the highway, is GLENTERRA VINE-YARDS (3897 Cobble Hill Road, 250-743-2330; open daily 11 a.m. to 6 p.m., noon to 5 p.m. in winter). Glenterra produces small lots of Pinot Gris, Chardonnay, Pinot Noir, Cabernet Franc, Meritage and a blend called Vivace from their vineyard.

Just across the highway is the DIVINO ESTATE WINERY (1500 Freeman Road, off Cowichan Bay Road, 250-743-2311; open

Friday and Saturday 1 to 5 p.m.). Ebullient and passionate about wine, scathing on the topic of what he regards as wine snobs, Joe Busnardo brought Divino's—an Okanagan winery since 1982—to the island in 1996. Most of his stock is from the Okanagan days, but he also makes Bay Bianco and Bay Russo from Cowichan Valley grapes. Half his 16 hectares are planted in kiwis, apples, cherries and thornless blackberries; grapevines take up the other half. Apples are for sale in August and September.

From Cowichan Bay Road (or turn from the highway onto Fisher Road and follow signs), follow Cherry Point Road to CHERRY POINT VINEYARDS (840 Cherry Point Road, 250-743-1272; open daily 10 a.m. to 6 p.m. for tasting and sales). From the time they established the vineyard in 1990, vintners Wayne and Helena Ulrich have done yeoman service in the building of a cot-

tage wine industry on the island. In addition to their main varieties, they planted a test vineyard in 1992 to see how 32 other varieties would adapt to the Cowichan climate. They have an art gallery and picnic grounds plus a pavilion for group events, conduct vineyard/winery tours on weekends, and host chamber music Sundays in the summer. Check their Website (*www.cherrypointvineyards.com*) for an events schedule.

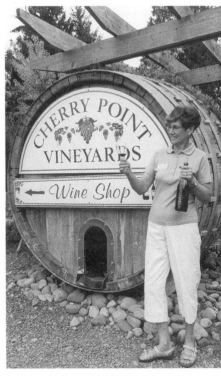

Their wines include Siegerrebe, Gewürztraminer, Pinot Gris, Agria, Pinot Noir, Ortega and their own blends, Valley Mist and Valley Sunset, as well as blackberry port.

Across the valley, on the west side of the highway, are three vineyards. Follow Lakeside Road from

Helena Ulrich samples some of Cherry Point's wine.

the highway or from Koksilah Road to Blue Grouse Road. BLUE GROUSE VINEYARDS AND WINERY (4365 Blue Grouse Road, 250-743-3834; open Wednesday through Sunday 11 a.m. to 5 p.m.) was the valley's second vineyard. Vintner Hans Klitz opened Blue Grouse in 1993, experimenting with 150 varieties before selecting cool-climate varieties that include Siegerrebe, Bacchus and Muller-Thurgau. The winery also offers Pinot Gris, Pinot Noir and Black Muscat. A charge for tasting is refundable on purchase. Check their Website (*www.bluegrousevineyards.com*).

Follow Glenora Road from Koksilah Road, or Allenby and Indian roads from Duncan, to discover VIGNETI ZANATTA (5039 Marshall Road, 250-748-2338; check by phone or at *www.zanatta.ca* for seasonal hours). Vigneti Zanatta is special: for its location on a 48-hectare farm the Zanattas bought in 1958; for the eclectic yard art around the farmhouse; for the other farm crops and produce; and for Vinoteca, the only vineyard restaurant on the island.

Vinoteca serves locally inspired food—"simple country cuisine" —some of it from the Zanatta farm, some from neighbouring producers, on the verandah and in the rooms of the 1903 farm-

Wines and cider from valley producers.

house. The restaurant is open March to December, Wednesday to Sunday noon to 5 p.m.; dinner is served Thursday to Saturday or by reservation.

Another kilometre or two up Marshall Road is the new kid on the block: GODFREY-BROWNELL VINEYARDS (4911 Marshall Road, 250-715-0504; call for hours; *www.gbvineyards.com*). Formerly a creative writing professor at the University of Victoria and computer guru, Dave Godfrey jokes that when he told his wife he wanted to own a vineyard when he retired, she had visions of Tuscany or Provence. Instead, they're at the edge of the Cowichan Valley, planting vines and serving wine in their picnic grounds. While they wait for their vines to mature, Godfrey-Brownell is making wines from Okanagan and Similkameen grapes; varieties include Chardonnay, Pinot Grigio and Pinot Noir.

ALDERLEA VINEYARDS (1751 Stamps Road, 250-746-7122; call for hours) is north of Duncan; follow Lakes Road to Stamps Road. Alderlea—the old name of Duncan—produces Pinot Gris, Pinot Noir, Pinot Auxerrois, Bacchus and Marechal Foch varietals, plus a white blend and a dark port-style wine.

Along the Way: West of the Highway

Down near Blue Grouse Vineyards, CALI FARM (2328 Koksilah Road, 250-746-6827; Monday through Saturday, dawn till dusk) specializes in organically grown basil, spinach, fat or skinny beets, tomatoes, salad mixes, garlic, onions—and walnuts and hazelnuts. Free-range eggs and chicken and lamb are also available.

CODE'S CORNER EMU FARM (5816 Menzies Road, 250-746-1593; by appointment) raises—what else?—emus. The world's second-largest birds at up to two metres tall and 70 kilos, they don't measure up to ostriches, which can stand more than a metre taller and weigh 180 kilos. Emus are flightless birds originating from Australia, where they have survived some 80 million years. Emu meat and emu oil are available, as are pre-booked farm tours.

KARIN'S COUNTRY (3899 Gibbins Road, 250-746-7191; call ahead) has eggs year-round, and seasonal chickens, turkeys, lamb, goat and pork, plus sausages. Farmyard animals abound here.

Valhalla Herb Farm

George, the sheep llama, stares over the fence at the intruders, then decides we are no danger to his charges—we're not dogs or cougars. So much the worse for us if we were: rouse Sir George Trincomale

Henri Andersen at work in the Valhalla kitchen.

or threaten his sheep and he'll kick you where it hurts.

George is the advance guard at the VALHALLA HERB FARM (3693 Gibbins Road, 250-748-1741; open April to October, Saturdays and Sundays 10 a.m. to 3 p.m.). Get past him, and you'll come upon a pleasantly dishevelled garden in front of a hundred-year-old farmhouse where Pat and Henri Andersen make preserves from the herbs they grow on their five hectares of land.

Much of the land has been left in its natural state, with animal channels preserved so the elk and deer that frequent the area can follow their usual paths. The sprawling gardens you see first reflect Pat's English background; they're the epitome of an English country garden. Behind the house are more formal gardens that reflect Henri's Danish heritage.

Both are filled with every variety of herb that can be imagined: more familiar herbs such as sage and lavender, but also exotic South American amaranth, bella cama—an oriental herb with a root like ginseng—and inula, a dandelion-like plant (though much taller) whose roots are recommended as a cure for coughing. Many other plants, such as a mulberry tree that was started from seed, a medlar tree with a fruit like a rose hip and zebra grass, thrive in the garden.

Valhalla reflects Pat's nursing and Henri's chef background. Henri began growing herbs when he couldn't find what he needed for his work in the kitchen. Pat has a special interest in herbal specifics and tonics. Henri rules in the kitchen, coming up with inventive herbal combinations for jellies, syrups, chutneys, herbal blends and herbal teas. The Andersens also sell dried herbs in season.

Along the Way: North and East of Duncan

A farm stand at COTTAGE FARM (6387 Lakes Road, 250-748-4630) looks over the valley to the saltwater beyond. Better known in the past for its holly, sold under the name of Amblecote Estate, this farm now sells vegetables, fruits and nuts, as well as eggs, jams, chutneys, pickles and flowers, at its green-roofed roadside stand. Free-range ducks and chickens are usually available; geese and beef can be ordered. SWEET PICKINS FARM (7087 Mays Road, off Herd Road, 250-701-4238) offers blueberries fresh in season, and frozen year-round.

Down in Maple Bay, Valerie and John Russell sell more than 50 varieties of garlic—soft-neck and hard-neck—from MAPLE BAY ORGANIC SEED GARLIC (6462 Pacific Drive, 250-746-7466; by appointment). RUSSELL FARMS (Highway 1 and Mt. Sicker Road, 250-246-4924; seven days a week year-round, 7 a.m. to 9 p.m. in summer, 8 a.m. to 7 p.m. off-season) has been supplying Cowichan Valley residents with fruits and vegetables for more than 50 years. The third generation of the family now runs the farm. At the market, you'll find strawberries, raspberries, tayberries and corn from the farm and a wide variety of other produce from other area and BC farms. Also on the site are a garden centre and a sit-down delicatessen.

At COWICHAN VALLEY COUNTRY HONEY (WESTCOTT FARM) (6691 Westcott Road, 250-748-5698; by chance or by appointment), you'll find two treats: honey from raspberry, blueberry and fireweed flowers and woolly Welsh Black Mountain sheep. The farm is home to 20 of the 250 of

Black Welsh Mountain sheep greet farmer Lorna Kearney at Westcott Farm.

this breed in Canada (fleeces are available). A Stonehenge mead kit that makes four litres of mead is also available.

Providence Farm

In 1858, the Sisters of St. Ann, a religious order founded in Quebec eight years earlier, arrived in Victoria to teach and to care for the sick. Over the next few decades, they founded schools and hospitals throughout British Columbia. In 1864, they established a mission school for native children near Duncan. Among other things, they taught native women how to knit spun wool from sheep that had been introduced into the valley in the 1850s. The production of famed Cowichan sweaters dates to that time.

A century later, the sisters and other Cowichan residents were seeking a new use for the 160-hectare St. Ann's property between the town and the sea, something that would uphold their own beliefs and their work for the community. Out of their desire to be open to the needs of the disabled and disadvantaged, Providence Farm was born. The farm's mission statement read, in part, "Trusting in Providence, we propose to create a faith centred

Garden beds and buildings at Providence Farm.

community that sees in the cycle of people caring for the soil and the soil nurturing the people—the Renewal of Life."

Providence is much more than a farm. The old buildings house an alternative school, a day program for adults with mental health difficulties, a therapeutic horticulture work program, a therapeutic riding program, a program for seniors in the early stages of Alzheimer's or dementia: the list of programs for the disabled and disadvantaged is almost endless. The St. Ann's garden, within the boundaries of the apple orchard the sisters established in the 1930s, welcomes art and photography groups as well as the seniors for whom it was originally intended.

Behind the house are a series of gardens where vegetables and fruits are grown and harvested, plus barns and buildings for live-stock, for processing and for sales. The PROVIDENCE FARM GENERAL STORE (1843 Tzouhalem Road, 250-746-8982; 9 a.m. to 3:30 p.m., seven days a week June to September; five days a week out of season) is stocked with farm produce, apple cider, preserves and crafts. Check out *www.providence.bc.ca* for more information on this unique community.

the island in between

THE STRIP OF COASTAL LAND from the north end of the Cowichan Valley to the southern reach of the Comox Valley looks like reluctant ground for farming. There's little enough flat land: the island mountains crowd in from the west and the ocean limits the land on the east. Chemainus is better known for logging and murals, Crofton for its pulp mill, Ladysmith and Nanaimo for old coal mines and new shopping centres. Parksville and Qualicum attract

Many a farmgate stand or sign is tucked away along the back roads near Errington and Coombs.

retirees to their sunny beaches and golf courses. Port Alberni, in a narrow valley at the head of an even narrower inlet, has lived mainly from its lumber mills and ocean fishing.

Yet the region has attracted its share of dreamers; scratch a dreamer and you're likely to find a farmer. We're not talking waving wheatfields here. But wherever there's a patch of pleasant fertile land, someone is bound to start a market garden; let the land be as much as a hectare in size and someone will contemplate a farm. And where there are market gardens or farms, farm stands exist.

From the time the Nanaimo coal mines opened in the 1850s, a market for farm produce existed in the area. Hay, oats and roots were in demand for coal-company horses. In the early days, residents depended on food from elsewhere, but as land was cleared, they were able to obtain potatoes and other vegetables locally. The area south of Nanaimo soon had a number of farms, both small and large. By the turn of the century, farmers here and to the north at Nanoose and to the west at Errington were producing tree fruits and soft fruits such as apples, pears, strawberries and raspberries.

Today, those same areas are home to a variety of market gardens, produce and poultry farms and larger dairy and beef farms. Change is frequent: I never know quite what I will find when I check out the back roads around Errington or near Cedar, but I know I will always find something intriguing. And at the farm

"

"*There are many small farms, well cleared and with good soil, between Nanaimo and Nanoose Bay.... Around Nanaimo, dairying is fairly profitable, but not nearly so profitable as it should be, because they fail to keep tally with their cows, or in other words, they fail to 'feed, breed, and weed,' especially the latter.... In two or three places in the district poultry breeding has been carried on with system.... We ought to hear from these men how they do it.... Beekeeping is being carried on more largely every year.... One man made $250 out of 32 colonies. Honey fetched 25 cents a pound this year.*"
—AGRICULTURAL CORRESPONDENT JOHN STEWART, 1902

markets, producers have time and willingness to chat about what's on the stand, the weather or the state of the world.

The Markets

- CEDAR FARMERS' MARKET, Sundays 10 a.m. to 2 p.m., mid-May to mid-October, at the Crow and Gate Pub.
- NANAIMO FARMERS' MARKET, Fridays 10 a.m. to 2 p.m., down-town by the Bastion, April to October.
- GABRIOLA ISLAND FARMERS' MARKET, Saturdays 10 a.m. to 2 p.m., May to Thanksgiving, Agricultural Association Hall, South Road.
- QUALICUM BEACH FARMERS' MARKET, Saturdays 9 a.m. to 12 p.m., Fir at Memorial, downtown, mid-May to October.
- ERRINGTON FARMERS' MARKET, Saturdays 10 a.m. to 1 p.m., Errington and Grafton roads, mid-May to early September.
- PORT ALBERNI FARMERS' MARKET, Saturdays 9 a.m. to 12 p.m., Alberni Harbour Quay, year-round.

The Route

The mid-island region includes a number of areas. SOUTH OF NANAIMO are the small farms near Ladysmith and Cedar. WEST OF NANAIMO, along Jingle Pot Road, are some small farms, a winery and a farm market. NORTH OF NANAIMO, follow Nanoose Bay Road for the best farmgating. The COOMBS–ERRINGTON area has long been the location of farms and farmgaters. The PARKSVILLE–QUALICUM BEACH area is home to both farmgaters and sellers of seafood. To the west, look for farm markets in the PORT ALBERNI area.

Along the Way: Ladysmith to Nanaimo

The Cedar Road veers east from Highway 19 north of Ladysmith Harbour. Yellow Point Road, in turn, departs from Cedar Road a few kilometres along. Turn right to ramble through countryside marked by farm fields and woods. The signs at the corner of Cedar and Yellow Point roads give you an idea of the variety you'll find on farm stands further along.

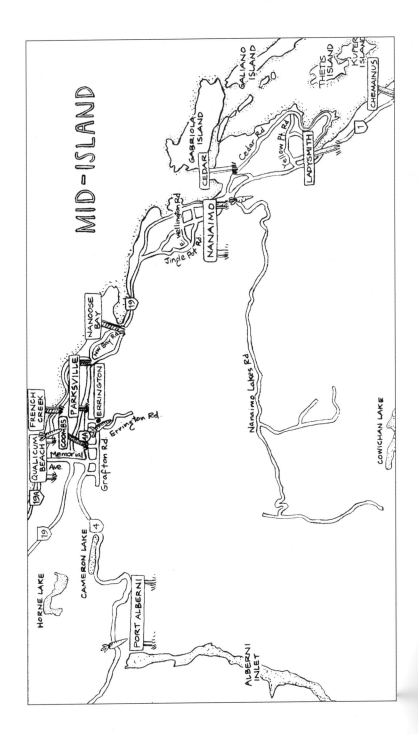

MID-ISLAND

Farm stands along Yellow Point Road offer a variety of produce.

MCNAB'S FARM (4613 Yellow Point Road) has a corn maze, a pumpkin patch, pony rides and corn and other produce for sale. LA FERME (4756 Yellow Point) offers organic eggs, chickens, blueberries and a variety of vegetables. Here, as elsewhere on the island, blueberries are becoming an ever more popular crop. Turn right on Michael Road on Friday, Saturday or Sunday for U-pick blueberries at 13601 Michael. You can pick up blueberry recipe books here too.

A nearby district is known as Cranberry, for the swamp cranberries that used to grow here, so it's nice to see that someone is keeping up the old tradition. Not swamp cranberries, though: these are the commercial variety for sale at G.D. KEEFER FARMS (4532 Yellow Point Road, 250-245-5283) with farmgate sales from late September through October and again at Christmastime. Grant

CRANBERRY HINTS

Grant Keefer says unsprayed cranberries need no preparation for the freezer: when the fruit is fresh and clean, place the berries in a bag and put them in the freezer. For cranberry sauce combine four parts cranberries, two parts sugar, one part water; boil about five minutes until the skins crack, then simmer until soft.

and Justine Keefer harvested their first cranberries in 2001, and are increasing their cranberry acreage each year. Though the majority of their berries go to a commercial buyer, they sell fresh cranberries at their Cranberry Cottage, along with sauces, chutneys, salsa and vinegar.

THE CRANBERRY HARVEST

If you fly in to Vancouver in October, you'll see bright burgundy fields below you: this is cranberry season. As the berries ripen, the fields are flooded, and the floating berries are herded in for harvest. Several Vancouver Island farms also now grow cranberries. Grant Keefer notes that cranberries grow on a vine something like ivy, completely covering the field. For commercial harvests, the Keefers flood their fields and, clothed in chest waders, follow a machine called a beater through the field, booming the cranberries over to one corner where they are pushed up a conveyor belt and into boxes. But the harvest of cranberries for fresh sales is different: they walk behind a machine that, with little fingers and belts, picks the cranberries for them. Then they can pass the berries through a blower that cleans off leaves and dirt, grade them, and offer them for sale.

Continue along Yellow Point, a pleasant road with farm fields on either side, interspersed with woods and ponds. Drop in at the Crow and Gate pub just before Cedar Road: this is the location of the weekly Cedar market. At the junction of Yellow Point and Cedar roads, look for signs that point towards area farm stands.

BHATTI'S BERRIES (2130 Holden-Corso Road, 250-722-2190; open daily in season; call for U-pick) has raspberries, blueberries and strawberries for sale at appropriate times of the year.

Easier to reach if you are travelling south, Spruston Road goes west from Highway 19 just before the Haslam Creek bridge. Watch for the Farm Fresh signs: down this road are a lavender farm and U-pick and ready-picked blueberries for sale.

Hazelwood Herb Farm

Richard White is working on a new batch of jellies in the kitchen at HAZELWOOD HERB FARM (13576 Adshead Road, 250-245-8007; 11 a.m. to 5 p.m. daily, April through September; 11 a.m. to 5 p.m., Friday through Sunday, October to Christmas Eve). He'll supply you with armfuls of basil if you order ahead, but Hazelwood's real business is in herb plants from their nursery and herb products from their kitchen. They make herb jellies, mustards and vinegars, beer bread mixes, herbal teas and herbal blends as well as the bath, skin care and other herbal products that are co-owner Jacynthe Dugas's province.

At the farm, you can take a self-guided tour through gardens where many varieties of herb are planted, check out the greenhouses for herb plants or visit the gift shop. Hazelwood also hosts special festivities on Mother's Day and Father's Day, a herb festival at the end of June, and two events in November. Check their Website (*www.hazelwoodherbfarm.com*) for details.

HINTS FOR GROWING BASIL FROM HAZELWOOD HERB FARM
Basil hates cool weather and can't take frost. A greenhouse is great if you have one. If not, follow these tips.

- When you buy the plant from a nursery, preferably around the end of May, harden it off: put it outside during the day, bring it back inside at night.
- Find a sheltered spot to plant your basil around the beginning of June. Use a plastic tunnel cover to shelter it from rain and wind and to keep it warm, especially at night, until the weather turns really warm.
- Feed it fish fertilizer every two weeks.
- Pinch back the flower stalks as they appear.

Along the Way: Behind Nanaimo

The Nanaimo bypass—the new Highway 19—makes it a little difficult to reach the web of back roads that lie between the city and Mount Benson. The easiest way to explore in this area is to

Vintner Harry Wolff at Chateau Wolff west of Nanaimo.

take one of the Jingle Pot Road exits from the highway, or to approach from the city itself.

Nanaimo, with its mining and logging heritage, seems an unlikely place for a winery. But winery there is: CHATEAU WOLFF (2534 Maxey Road, 250-753-9669; open Saturdays and Sunday, 11 a.m. to 6 p.m.) produces Pinot Blanc, Pinot Noir and a red dessert wine. Half the pleasure of visiting the winery comes from chatting with—or more likely, listening to—Harry Wolff, the winery's exuberant owner who gleefully cuts down any pretentious wine talk.

Almost across the street is ARGYLE FARM ORGANIC PRODUCE (2403 Maxey, 250-754-9272; open Saturdays 10 a.m. to 6 p.m., year-round), with carrots, garlic, potatoes, lettuce, beets and other seasonal vegetables, including potatoes, endive, leeks and lettuce in winter.

Along Jingle Pot Road, in this still surprisingly rural area, is a newcomer to the farmgate market business: look for chickens underfoot and a petting farm at the SHADY MILE FARM MARKET (3452 Jingle Pot Road, 250-729-3801). Shady Mile brings in much of its produce from elsewhere on the island and mainland, but also stocks local treats such as Lantzville-grown figs.

Along the Way: North of Nanaimo

Up at the north end of Nanoose Bay, North West Bay Road heads east to circle the peninsula from here to Parksville. Look for a great variety of made-on-the-premises dry, smoked and fresh sausages, including a spicy gypsy stick just right for on-the-road nibbling, at HUG'S LITTLE SAUSAGE HOUSE (2348 North West Bay Road, 250-468-1743; open Tuesday through Friday 10 a.m. to 6 p.m., Saturday 10 a.m. to 4 p.m.).

Nanoose Edibles

It seems an odd place to find a farm as good as this one, amid the cow pastures and logging cuts of the Nanoose peninsula. But when Barbara and Lorne Ebell chose this land, they knew what they were

At Nanoose Edibles, the bed of an old and fertile river delta has been transformed into a market garden.

doing: he had a PhD in plant physiology, she was from a farm background, and both wanted to farm at some point in their lives. Once their kids were grown up and gone, they converted four of their nine hectares on and around an ancient riverbed to an organic market garden. Spend some time touring the garden here, and you'll notice a steady stream of cars from as far south as Nanaimo and as far north as Qualicum Beach bringing loyal customers to stock up on fresh vegetables and fruits.

The Ebells have kept the sheltering belts of trees that were there when they bought the property, deepened an existing pond for irrigation, and tried to grow their crops within the limitations of the best arable land on the property.

NANOOSE EDIBLES (1960 Stewart Road, 250-468-2332; Tuesday through Sunday 11 a.m. to 6 p.m.) does about half its sales to the restaurant business, half from the farm or at the Qualicum Beach market. Because their location is reasonably sheltered, they have a long growing season and can experiment with growing vegetables year-round. Their winter produce includes kale, collards and other greens that can put up with the cooler climate. Phone ahead for winter hours.

"We grow about everything," says Barbara, who is a fervent advocate of organic produce. "We have the most fun at the farm market, but we also sell here; we're growing for people in the neighbourhood."

As well as such field vegetables as eggplant, broccoli and half a dozen varieties of beets, they grow greens, tomatoes and peppers in their greenhouses, plus tree and soft fruits and flowers. Chickens squawk softly in their henhouses: eggs are available.

BARBARA EBELL'S BEST GARDENING TIP
"Go to the library and look up winter gardening. You'll find some good recommendations and tips. Nearly everything in the West Coast Seeds winter catalogue will thrive on Vancouver Island. You need good-quality soil and shelter from the wind and rain— but you can grow your own salads year-round."

Along the Way: Errington-Coombs Area

You'll need a map for this area, so stop at the Parksville Infocentre, at the south end of Parksville, and ask for the Oceanside Farm Products Guide, an eight-panel listing of area farms and produce. The farm guide will bring you up to date on who's still in business, who's selling what. Then head for Highway 4, the Coombs Road, and turn south on Bellevue, to wander Grafton and Errington roads, plus various others. If it's a summer Saturday, you can drop in at the Errington market; on other days, keep a sharp eye out for alpacas in the field and produce on the stands.

The ERRINGTON FARMERS' MARKET (Errington Road at Errington Hall, 250-248-5404; Saturdays 10 a.m. to 1 p.m., May to September) is well worth a visit. It's unique for its location, in the shade of old Douglas firs and cedars. Friends and acquaintances from around the area meet here to chat, have a coffee and sit at the picnic tables or on the steps of the hall. The pies from Checkergrass Farm go early, usually in the first 20 minutes after the market opens. Crafts and garden plants are on sale here, as well as every kind of produce and a variety of meats, poultry and processed products.

In the shady setting of the Errington Market.

John Olsen of Unicorn Farm displays garlic braids.

UNICORN FARM (1430 Errington Road, near Grafton Road, 250-248-2272; weekends and holidays, 9 a.m. to 6 p.m.) specializes in garlic and garlic products; you may also find other products here, such as eggs, blueberries and vegetables.

TIGER LILY FARM (1692 Errington Road, 10 a.m. to 4 p.m. daily) has eggs for sale but is also a good farm stop for children, with a petting farm and pony rides. SILVERMEADOWS FARMS (2040 Swayne Road, 250-248-2808; corn only; watch for the sign in corn season) must be one of the prettiest farms in the region, with its views over the farm pond and fields to the mountains beyond. Check out the koi pond in the market building where Silvermeadows sells its corn. While you're in the neighbourhood, look over the fence at WESTWOOL ALPACAS (1898 Swayne Road) to see these exotic, long-necked, soft-wooled relatives of the camel, from the South American altiplano.

Drive along nearby Grafton Road, through a pleasant rural landscape, to discover a variety of seasonal farm stands offering products such as eggs, emu oil and herbs.

GARLIC LORE

Thinking of building a pyramid? Labourers who built the Great Pyramid of Giza were fed garlic, radishes and onions—an inscription on the pyramid tells us how much these strength-enhancers cost. And when the children of Israel left Egypt for the wilderness, they lamented the loss of, among other things, cucumbers, melons, leeks, onions—and, of course, garlic.

Did you know that alpacas love to travel and will fit in the family mini-van? Or that they don't have upper teeth and must make do with a hard dental pad? Now you do.

Regatta Gardens

In darker days, one of the worst-tasting foods was strawberries out of their all-too-brief season. Red-painted styrofoam would have tasted better. Then along came everbearing, and then day-neutrals. Now, sweet, juicy strawberries are available from June through mid-September.

REGATTA GARDENS (1990 Alberni Highway, 250-248-9240; daily in August; U-pick Tuesdays, Thursdays and Saturdays, 9:30 a.m. till sold out) sell both the traditional June berries—the variety they raise is Rainier—and a sweet and tasty day-neutral called Tribute that has a first flush of production in June and a main season from August through early September.

Barry and Sylvia Neden have operated this farm for 15 years. "We're the twentieth-century pioneers here," says Sylvia. "We

Picking strawberries at Regatta Gardens.

cleared the land and put it into production." Graduates of Olds Agricultural College in Alberta, they came back home to where Barry was born and raised. They started out with vegetables, then moved into soft fruits.

They have garnered a big following for their Tribute berries, a variety they chose carefully, after checking out research conducted in the Fraser Valley. "They favour the wild strawberry—lots of flavour and a little bit tart." Regulars know that they should be there early on U-pick days to make sure they get their berries.

Regatta also sells raspberries in July and vegetables in season: "staples, not exotics—it's like an oversized family garden."

WHAT'S A DAY-NEUTRAL?
Strawberries traditionally respond to the length of the day. Regular strawberry plants—known as Junebearers—produce runners in summer's long days, initiate flower buds (which are dormant over the winter) in autumn's short days and fruit in the following spring. Everbearers are of two types. The first, usually known simply as everbearers, fruit on summer buds in autumn and on autumn buds the following spring. Day-neutral strawberries, plants that don't care about the length of the daylight, produce flower buds and fruit continuously, as long as the temperature remains below 29°C and above 2°C. Day-neutrals are much beloved of strawberry growers on the west coast, because they supply strawberries well into September.

Along the Way: Parksville–Qualicum Beach

Just south of Parksville on the old highway is CORMIE'S MARKET (Island Highway at Riverside Road, 250-248-2733; open daily), where produce from the Cormies' three hectares and three greenhouses, as well as from other local, BC and more distant farms, is on sale. The Cormie farm has been in operation since 1953.

Most of the farms in the Parksville Qualicum area sell at the Qualicum Beach market on Saturday mornings. MINDI'S FARM

Fishing boats docked at French Creek, near the seafood market.

MARKET (797 Qualicum Road, 250-752-9221) sells produce from its own farm and other local and Fraser Valley farms.

A market not to be missed is FRENCH CREEK SEAFOODS (1097 Lee Road, at the French Creek dock north of Parksville; 250-248-7100; open daily). The market shares the waterfront with a seafood processing plant and some of the remaining fishing boats that ply

A MARINADE FOR SALMON OR HALIBUT
Use this for almost any firm-textured fish.

½ cup olive oil
2 Tbsp. soya sauce
¼ cup whiskey or dark rum
¼ tsp. pepper
1 Tbsp. brown sugar
2 cloves garlic
1 tsp. salt
optional: 1 tsp. chopped ginger, or fresh dill, or lemon juice
Marinate at room temperature for at least 30 minutes.

—COURTESY FRENCH CREEK SEAFOOD

Dorper-Katahdin hair sheep at Evans Acres.

the waters between the island and the mainland. All kinds of local seafood, including salmon candy and various flavours of smoked salmon prepared by a Port Alberni processor, are available from the store.

Evans Acres

You could understand a child wanting to run in three directions at once here: fuzzy ducklings in a pen are being cradled by the farmers' sons, a tiny goat is bleating near the farm stand and a whole flock of funny-looking sheep are just a field away. But it's the corn maze they came for, and after a few fond looks backward at the goat, they head across the road and disappear into the three-metre-high cornstalks.

EVANS ACRES (250 Hilliers Road North, 250-752-0749) has that sense of a good old-fashioned farm, with acres of pasture and picturesque barns, the corn field, the farm animals and a real feeling of space on 140 hectares west of Qualicum Beach. Bob and Marnie Evans have been running the heritage property for four years now. Evans Acres is part of what used to be the 400-hectare Arrowsmith Farm, well-known throughout the region for such farming feats as supplying frogs' legs to Victoria's Empress Hotel.

"I love doing this, because people don't get to go to farms much any more," notes Marnie as she describes the corn maze they started in 1998. "My husband is a fanatic maze person, and when he read about corn mazes in England, well...." The Evans Acres corn maze is a treasure hunt, where walkers decipher pathways that lead them to such things as a pumpkin, a wagon wheel, a goose and an old-fashioned fire extinguisher.

What about those funny-looking sheep, animals that seem to have just been sheared no matter what time of year you visit? They are Dorper-Katahdin hair sheep, a wool-less cross-breed—meat animals that never need shearing.

Along the Way: Port Alberni

The Beaver Valley, west of Port Alberni, holds most of the area's farms. A trip along Beaver Creek Road in summer is a pleasant drive through rural country and may turn up some farm stands. NAESGAARD FARM MARKET (5681 River Road at Mary Street, 250-723-3622; open daily year-round) is the best known of the city's markets. On the way west out of town, it is well-marked with signs and is almost always busy. Among the offerings: peas, beans, tomatoes, corn, carrots from the Naesgaard farm, as well as Okanagan fruit, Port Alberni honey and other local products.

Naesgaard's Farm Market in Port Alberni.

Farther west, FARMER BILL'S COUNTRY MARKET (7676 Pacific Rim Highway, 250-723-7700; 9 a.m. to 6 p.m. daily, June through October) offers corn, pumpkins, cucumbers and squash from the farm—a large part of which has been in the Thomson family for a hundred years—as well as other local farm products. Also at the farm market or on the farm: a corn maze, farm tours and special events, including a haunted barn and hay wagon rides in October.

comox valley

I WAS WHEELING ALONG the back roads west of Courtenay one August day when I saw a sign: strawberries for sale. In those days, local strawberries were strictly limited to June and July. Yet down that winding country road, farmer Dick McGinnis was growing berries of surpassing sweetness and was more than happy to discourse on the merits of his new day-neutrals.

Thus began my continuing love affair with the produce of the Comox Valley. Unlike my home area in Saanich, foraging here was never simple: there was no handy list of producers, complete with

Cabbages in a Comox Valley field.

maps, or farm markets around every corner. Instead, the customer in search of farmgate products had to wander the roads through the rolling farm fields, watching for signs that advertised lettuce or quail or eggs or apples. There were always surprises: a farmer or a gardener who was happy to experiment and put the results of that experiment up for sale.

McGinnis, ever seeking new opportunities, has gone on to other plans and newer crops. But the owners of On Line Farms, one of my other happy finds on that trip, still follow their biodynamic philosophy, and I still find surprises when I drive the back roads: someone cultivating thornless blackberries here, someone serving beautiful blueberries over ice cream there.

The Comox Valley has a long agricultural history. Though the first non-native settlers came here to mine coal, they soon discovered the fertility of the fields they cleared. By the turn of the century, correspondent J.A. Halliday could report: "The farmers here are contented and prosperous; we have many privileges, schools, churches, post offices, etc., but are dissatisfied with our mail service . . . . Soil is good; climate healthy; some winters no snow. There

―――――――――― 66 ――――――――――

"The soil is rich and the surrounding country beautiful. There is none of these extremes of bad soil as in the Cowichan District. . . . Monster potatoes, onions as large as Spanish ones, parsnips, wheat and oats full headed, and sound turnips, splendid butter & milk are productions of this most beautiful valley. During our visit hay was being cut in the meadows at the river's mouth for the Victoria market & the farms are capable of producing everything a farm can. I have rarely or ever, even in England, seen more lovely situations for homes to men willing to go to their work with heart and spirit—believing in the Country and its prosperity—a subject not now requiring a great amount of faith. Beans are said not to prosper so well."

—ROBERT BROWN, VANCOUVER ISLAND
EXPLORING EXPEDITION, 1864

are about 80 persons engaged in agriculture, who cultivate about 6,000 acres of land."

Now, as then, dairying is a big part of agriculture in the valley, with a cheesemaking company garnering awards for its innovative production. Small fruits, apples, vegetables of all kinds show up on stands and at market. The market at the Comox Valley fairgrounds is one of the best on the island, renowned for the wide choice of products, from exotic greens to gnarled wasabi to venison chops, and for the friendliness of both sellers and buyers. And now, as then, farmgating in the Comox Valley is an unpredictable, rewarding and pleasant way to spend a summer's day.

The Markets

- CAMPBELL RIVER DOWNTOWN MARKET, Sundays 10 a.m. to 1 p.m., June through October, Tyee Plaza.
- COMOX VALLEY FARMERS' MARKET, Saturdays 9 a.m. to noon, mid-April to mid-October, Exhibition Ground, Headquarters Road; Wednesdays 9 a.m. to noon, mid-April to mid-October, 4th Street and Duncan, Courtenay.
- HORNBY ISLAND FARMERS' MARKET, Wednesdays and Saturdays 11 a.m. to 2 p.m., July and August, behind the Community Hall.
- QUADRA ISLAND FARMERS' MARKET, Saturdays 10 a.m. to 2 p.m., May through September, behind the credit union on West Road.
- TEXADA FARMERS' MARKET, Sundays 12:30 to 2:30 p.m., mid-June to early October, Gillies Bay.

The Route

The valley widens out from Qualicum Bay NORTH TO COURTENAY, with oyster farmers and a few farmgaters along the way and a cheesemaker's store in town. Farmers and market gardeners are found on the COMOX PENINSULA east of the Island Highway, along the back roads WEST OF COURTENAY and on either side of the highway NORTH OF COURTENAY, as well as on the NORTHERN

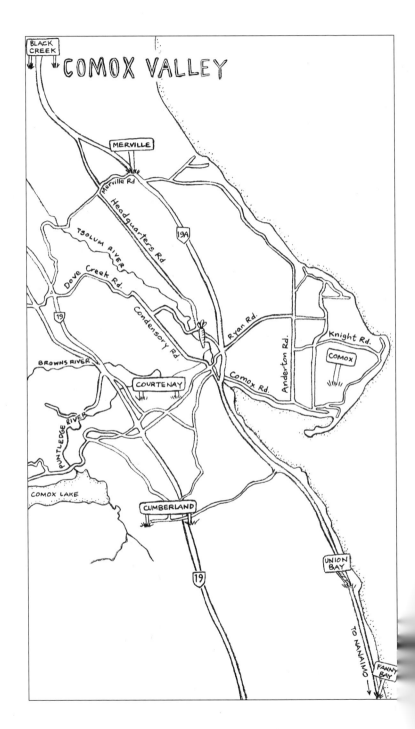

GULF ISLANDS. The route follows Comox, Lazo, Knight, Little
River and Anderton roads near Comox; continues on Waveland,
Bates and Coleman roads to the highway, then farther north;
explores Headquarters, Condensory and Dove Creek roads and the
surrounding area west of the highway.

PRODUCT LIST, COMOX VALLEY, 1902
Potatoes, carrots (but not many, "owing to expense of keeping
clean and harvesting"), mangolds, all other vegetables for home
use; onions at 2 cents a pound; gooseberries, blackberries and red
currants; many varieties of apples, including "20-Oz Pippin,"
Gravenstein, Maiden's Blush, Gloria Mundi and Siberian crab;
pears, including Beurre d'Anjou, Souvenir de Congres and
Clapp's Favorite; plums ("most orchards have a few trees"). Dairy
and beef cattle, pigs and poultry ("several here depend entirely on
their poultry for subsistence") were also raised at the turn of the
century. Among the problems: the absence of a Thistle Inspector,
clearing land, the need for more creameries, the want of agricultural instruction, and the carelessness of campers and men with
their pipes who caused forest fires.
—REPORT OF THE DEPARTMENT OF AGRICULTURE, 1902

Along the Way: North to Courtenay

North of Qualicum Beach, you can either go fast—cutting over to
the Inland Island Highway and skipping all the interesting
details—or go farmgating, by taking the old highway, now known
as 19A, through the seaside communities of Qualicum Bay, Fanny
Bay, Union Bay and Royston. Keep an eye out along the way for
seasonal farm stands and signs; seasonal vegetables and eggs seem
to be the most popular items that area gardeners/farmers sell.

But the real joy along this stretch of road that borders the ocean
is the shellfish suppliers. Baynes Sound curls between Vancouver
Island and Denman Island, providing a protected area ideal for cultivating oysters and clams: the sound produces more than a third of

Oyster shells are piled deep at Baynes Sound Oysters, near Fanny Bay.

BC's commercial oysters and more than half of its clams. MAC'S OYSTERS (seafront between Fanny and Union Bay, 250-335-2233, 250-335-2129; open daily) was the first commercial oyster farm in the area, dating back to the 1950s. They sell oysters and clams, in the shell or shucked. BAYNES SOUND OYSTERS (seafront just south

FAMOUS OYSTERS

Fanny Bay Oysters are famed far from home: you'll find them on the menu as far away as San Francisco, Philadelphia and Japan. They are Pacific oysters—not a native variety, but introduced from Japan to Ladysmith waters in 1912. In Baynes Sound, they are grown in net bags on racks in the intertidal zone and harvested when they are 8 to 10 centimetres in diameter. They are said to be medium saline in taste, with a firm texture and a fruity finish. Can't wait till you get home to find out what "fruity finish" actually means? The Fanny Bay Inn, on the waterfront highway just south of the bay, always has oysters on the menu.

of Union Bay, 250-335-2111) sells oysters and clams, in the shell or shucked; they can also sell you cold packs to keep your shellfish fresh until you get home. Fanny Bay Oysters is the largest producer of oysters. Their retail outlet is not at their processing plant, but at THE SEAFOOD SHOP (at the Buckley Bay–Denman Island ferry landing, below the gas station; 250-335-1198; Saturday to Thursday 9 a.m. to 6 p.m.; Friday 9 a.m. to 9 p.m.). The Seafood Shop also sells clams and other seafood, such as scallops, shrimp, prawns, cod, sole, snapper, salmon and crab, when available.

IRONWOOD ORGANIC FARM (8301 South Island Highway, Fanny Bay, 250-335-2557; no formal hours, March to December) produces everything organic from arugula to zucchini. They suggest that Tuesdays and Fridays are the best days to drop by, since they are picking for the Comox Valley market on those days and are more likely to have a cooler full of vegetables.

DEAR ARUGULA

It sounds like it should be a girl's name, or the name of an island in the Pacific, but arugula is, instead, a leafy green vegetable of Mediterranean origin, shaped something like a deeply indented oak leaf. Aromatic, with a spicy taste that has tones from licorice to peanut butter (or so its devotees say), it was grown as long ago as Roman times for its leaves and for its seed, used to flavour oils. It was also an ingredient in ancient aphrodisiacs—but then, what wasn't?

Natural Pastures Cheese

Maybe it was a surprise to other Canadian cheesemakers, but Vancouver Island aficionados of NATURAL PASTURES CHEESE (635 McPhee Ave., Courtenay, 250-334-4422; Monday to Friday 1 to 4 p.m.) just nodded when they learned that the Courtenay company had snaffled three top prizes at the Canadian Cheese Grand Prix, the only cheesemakers outside Ontario and Quebec to be so honoured. Out here, we'd been nibbling away at Comox

Natural Pastures' Edgar Smith and Mary Ann Hyndman Smith greet cheese-lovers at the valley market.

Camembert and NATURAL PASTURES' other cheeses since they began producing in 2001.

Government regulations keep visitors out of the actual cheese-making area on Courtenay's McPhee Avenue—but it's well worth a visit to their retail outlet at the cheese plant to gaze at the wheels of cheese in the ageing room and sample soft and semi-hard cheeses: Brie, Camembert, Verdelait, Boerenkass, blue Cheddar and Amsterdammer, all made from area milk.

Natural Pastures has its origins in the Comox dairy farm owned by Edgar Smith, the only designated heritage dairy farm in Canada. On Smith's farm, cows graze on natural pasture—no pesticides, antibiotics or growth hormones—and are outside for most of the year. Proud of his 350 Holsteins, Jerseys, Jersey crosses, Dutch belted and Normandy cows, some five years ago Smith was looking for a way to add value to his operation. Meanwhile, Rick Adams was enchanted by the artisan cheese he sampled on a trip to New Zealand. Smith met Adams, and Natural Pastures was born under the guidance of cheesemaker Paul Sutter.

The cheeses are made at Natural Pastures in Courtenay, west of the downtown area, where you can purchase various NP cheese (not all varieties are available at all times) and pick up cheese recipes and hints. The cheeses are also available at various outlets on Vancouver Island; phone for details.

CRANBERRY AND CURDS

Natural Pastures publicist Mary Ann Hyndman Smith suggests spreading spicy cranberry marmalade over a wheel of Natural Pastures Brie and baking the Brie in a 150°C (300°F) oven for 8 to 12 minutes. Cool slightly, and serve with crackers and apple and pear slices. Natural Pastures also makes cheese curds, those squeaky cubes that evolve early in the cheesemaking process and that were made famous by Miss Muffet. Sprinkle them into soups, salads, casseroles or chili; melt them over nachos—or eat them fresh. Or make a cross-cultural Quebecois poutine with West Coast curds: sprinkle the curds on hot French fries and cover with hot gravy. Opinions vary about the results: it's either *délicieuse* or *épouvantable*.

Along the Way: The Comox Area

Across the Courtenay River, north from the town of Comox, farm fields stretch towards the Comox Air Base and the regional airport. The fields do double duty here: they support crops and cows, but they are also home in winter and spring to some 3,000 trumpeter swans. Working together, wildlife experts and farmers have devised ways to feed the swans on crops planted especially for them in harvested vegetable fields while keeping them from destroying pasture cover in cattle fields.

To find farm stands near Comox, follow Comox Avenue to Lazo and Knight roads, continue on Military Row and Little River Road, then turn left successively onto Wilkinson, Ellenor and Anderton to return to the centre of Comox.

Along Knight Road, you'll find seasonal farm stands offering a

Squash and pumpkins at Acacia Acres.

variety of produce. Farther on, stop at ACACIA ACRES (1539 Little River Road, 250-339-6816) from June to October for a wide variety of products. In late summer and fall, you'll find apples and some 20 varieties of squash. It's particularly pleasant, after a hot summer's day spent foraging, to drop by BLUEHAVEN FARM (2046 Idiens Way, off Anderton Road, 250-339-4751; 11 a.m. to 7 p.m. Sunday and Monday, 9 a.m. to 7 p.m. Tuesday and Wednesday, 11 a.m. to 9 p.m. Thursday through Saturday). You can pick your own blueberries from the hectare of blueberry bushes and sample fresh-picked blueberries folded into vanilla ice cream or blueberry cheesecake and other desserts.

Sieffert's Farm Market

Charlene Sieffert is delighted that I want to photograph the Sieffert farm, the source of most of the produce sold at SIEFFERT'S FARM MARKET (746 Knight Road, 7 days a week 10 a.m. to 5:30 p.m.). She never tires of the beauty of the fields green and golden in the sunshine, with the mountain glaciers rising far beyond. We jump into her pickup truck and do the tour, down bumpy tracks past fields of carrots and cabbages and other field crops, looking for an elusive irrigation spray that would, she says, just make the best photo.

We don't find any irrigation running—but it's easy to see why the Sieffert family has been farming this land for generations and why Charlene and Bob's kids are happy to work on the farm. Things have changed, though, since the earliest days of growing basic products in field plots. As we arrive back at the roadside market on Knight Road, Charlene heads for a greenhouse where an

VEGETABLES UNDER GLASS

British Columbia's greenhouse growers are becoming well known for the quality of the produce they grow. Though Vancouver Island has nothing like the plethora of greenhouses in the Lower Mainland, a number of island farmers either specialize in greenhouse growing or expand their range by growing specialty products in greenhouses.

Long English cucumbers, smooth-skinned and seedless, are a favourite crop, as are tomatoes and peppers. The plants are grown, not in soil, but hydroponically, with the roots supported by sawdust or rock wool. Growers control pests biologically by introducing predator insects to eat pest insects: good bugs eat bad bugs.

alarm howls: the temperature has risen and threatens the greenhouse tomatoes and long English cucumbers.

Farm markets come and go in the Comox Valley. But Sieffert's Market is an institution, with vegetables of all sorts from these fields and from land the family owns or leases in the valley. What

The fields at the Sieffert farm stretch out towards the mountains behind Comox.

exactly do they grow and sell? Sieffert smiles. "Just about everything. We don't grow asparagus or celery or artichokes—but
almost everything else."

Patron Orchard
Well, of course PATRON ORCHARD (1507 Philmonte Road, 250-
338-1912; daily 1 to 5 p.m., year-round) has patrons—but that's not
how it got its name. Pat and Ronnie Murphy bought over a hectare
of land here in 1970, then started planting apple trees some
14 years later. Though their son, Robert, has taken over much of
the orchard's operation, you'll still find the founders at the Comox
Valley Market on Saturdays.

The orchard contains some 18 or 19 apple varieties. Ronnie's
favourite is Gravenstein: she eats four a week of this tart-sweet-
crisp old-timer. You can sit at a picnic table and eat your apple, or
wander through the orchard. Also available year-round are apple
juice in sizes from .25 to 4 litres and Mrs. Murphy's apple pies.

Apple trees at Patron Orchard.

Time to relax at the valley market.

Comox Valley Farmers' Market

Small farmers and market gardeners often have a problem: they want to sell direct to the consumer but find they can't take the time away from growing to provide good service—and they can't afford to hire someone else to do it. And it's not as easy now as it used to be to trust that people who drop by an untended stand will leave the right amount of money—or that no one will make off with the cash box.

Back in 1992, Comox Valley farmers met to talk about setting up a market that would help solve these problems. In May, 12 producers set up tailgates and tables to sell their vegetables and fruit. Early photographs of the COMOX VALLEY FARMERS' MARKET (Saturday mornings at the Exhibition Grounds) show wide spaces between the sellers.

Fast-forward 10 years. Overwhelmed, the original volunteers have given way to a market manager; the number of sellers has increased to more than 50 and space is at a premium. Baked goods, meats, cheeses, preserves and seafoods are now part of the line-up, all produced, processed or grown in the Comox Valley. A second market, on Wednesdays, and a Christmas market that runs in November and December have been added to the schedule. Farmgating in the valley can be hit-or-miss, but the market always delivers.

Long-time Saturday market-goers arrive sharp at 9 a.m., well aware that the best produce or the most sought-after bread will be gone by 9:30. Shopping bags and baskets bulging, they can then take a seat at a picnic table to listen to a musical group perform, lean against a hay bale in the sunshine or catch up on the news with other market regulars.

WHAT'S A WASABI?

It's a rock group, a film, a paddling club, a design firm. But the real and original wasabi is a gnarled greenish-brown rhizome or underground stem. It's grown in the Comox Valley by Hazelmere Farms and available at the valley market. Once you've bought it, what to do with it? Wasabi, or Japanese horseradish, is most familiar to Canadians as the fiery green paste that comes with sushi (though real wasabi lovers suggest that much of that paste in North America is actually powdered, coloured horseradish). It can be kept for up to a month, immersed in water in the refrigerator (change the water every few days) or frozen. To use, scrub the stem gently, sharpen like a pencil, then grate with a fine grater.

Since the tenth century, the Japanese have been considering the medical uses of wasabi; among the possibilities are helping to treat or prevent blood clotting, asthma and, perhaps, cancer—as well as preventing tooth decay.

If you're adventurous, you could seek (though not in the Comox Valley) a candy made from dark chocolate with wasabi, Japanese ginger and black sesame seeds.

Along the Way: Back Roads Behind Courtenay

Between the old Island Highway—19A—and the new inland highway—19—back roads criss-cross on either side of the Tsolum River. A good map is helpful here: if you don't know the roads and bridges, you may end up thinking you just can't get there from here. Try *Maps of the Comox Valley*, on sale at the infocentre in Courtenay.

Dove Creek Road usually has some small roadside stands with vegetables, plus U-pick blueberry farms. Follow Piercey Road to Greaves Crescent, then to tiny Darcy Road for NATURE'S WAY FARM (4905 Darcy Road, 250-338-9765; open daily 11 a.m. to 6 p.m., July through mid-September). Its farm stand has, in season, organic vegetables, raspberries, strawberries and blueberries, including Darrow blueberries. These are the largest and some of the tastiest around—tart/sweet and worth the extra that they cost. The variety, rare on Vancouver Island, was named for Dr. George Darrow, referred to as America's foremost authority on small fruits.

Headquarters Road, on the east side of the river, runs through dairy fields and horse farms, with some seasonal stands offering produce along the way.

DeeKayTee Ranch

The "farm" in farm markets usually means fruits and vegetables. DEEKAYTEE (6301 Headquarters Road, 250-337-5553; open weekends year-round 9 a.m. to 4 p.m.) is different: Dan and Maggie Thran's operation produces beef fed on pasture, forage and grain

The DeeKayTee market on Headquarters Road.

without hormones, feed additives or processed feed. It is, they say, "pure and simple beef."

Danny grew up on the farm, which has been in the family since 1924. He and Maggie have been raising beef cattle for 30 years; now they are raising poultry as well. The farm market is a new venture, housed in an attractive wooden building at the front of their ranch. Inside, you'll find a variety of beef cuts, eggs, chickens and turkeys, as well as produce from a dozen local farmers and such things as jam from the Jam Lady, fleeces, wool, fresh baking and herbs.

The Thrans also rent out two log cabins on their ranch where you can try a farm experience with wood heat, propane hot water, solar-powered lights and no telephone.

Along the Way: North to Campbell River

North of Courtenay, east of the North Island Highway, various farmers and market gardeners sell produce from stands and operate U-picks. Tired of getting your clothes and yourself ripped up by wild blackberry thorns? In August, check out 5923 LOXLEY (off Coleman Road near Bates Beach; 250-334-4377) for thornless blackberry picking. Off Hardy Road, the OUTBACK EMUZING RANCH (2301 Clarke Road, 250-338-8227) offers a look at these gigantic birds and the products from them.

Clearing land north of town was no picnic, and the soil was less fertile than that nearer the Courtenay area rivers. But would-be farmers persisted, and driving the back roads—and the Old Island Highway—north from town turns up a variety of farm stands and

 SAVING SEEDS

Heather Mills, from Ployart Farms, tells how to save tomato seeds for your garden. "Save the earliest and the best fruit from each plant for seed. Let the fruit rot. Take the seeds out and mix them with sand, to clean off the pulp. Then screen the seeds from the sand for next year's planting."

markets; watch for signs offering such things as rhubarb, apple sauce and roasting chickens.

North along the highway, check out DEVONSHIRE FARM (5147 Island Highway, 250-334-4552; daily year-round, daylight to dark). Devonshire produces mainly root crops—"We don't do anything leafy," says owner Robin Woodrow—including potatoes, carrots, turnips, onions and beets, as well as corn and dill cucumbers.

Just north of Black Creek, turn on to Ennis, then Ployart, roads to check out two farm stands, including PLOYART ROAD FARM (2230 Ployart Road, Saturdays, 10 a.m. to 5 p.m.), with vegetables including tomatoes,

Tom Walton hoists bags of dill cucumbers at Devonshire Farm.

beets, potatoes, chard and zucchini, as well as preserves, pies and lavender sachets. Just to the north, SUNSHINE ACRES POULTRY (8486 North Island Highway, Black Creek, 250-337-8157; call ahead) provides eggs, chickens, Cornish hens and turkeys. TWIN PEAKS GAME FARM (8083 Island Highway, 250-337-2078; call ahead) sells fallow deer venison, wild boar meat, lamb and beef.

On Line Farms

Look at a photo from the early days of the valley market, and ON LINE FARMS (corner Hardy Road and North Island Highway, 250-338-8342; daily 9:30 a.m. to 6 p.m., May to October) will be there, one of the first organic farms in the region. But there's always something new at On Line. Owners Lang Price and Marjon de Jong work on biodynamic farming principles and have now introduced Flowforms to their 10 hectares of land, a hectare of it used for vegetable production.

Biodynamic farming means looking at soil as a living system; it's a concept that can be as simple, on a practical level, as the skilful use of organic matter, and as complex, on a spiritual level, as taking into account the forces of the cosmos. Marjon de Jong, struggling to find a definition that doesn't take three pages or 30 minutes, says, "It's feeding the soil, not the plants. Of course, that applies to organic farming as well...."

But you won't find Flowforms on your average organic farm. Between On Line's farm market and the greenhouse, water flows through a series of concrete forms. The forms replace the hours of hand stirring that was required for the preparations that On Line puts on its fields. The movement of the water can be mesmerising. "When we started, the staff took their coffee breaks out there—and right away, they were spending half an hour watching and listening, instead of 15 minutes."

On Line produces what people want most, and that means carrots, potatoes and onions. But they also have a flare for the unusual, from shingeku (an edible chrysanthemum) and totsoi (loose-leaf Chinese cabbage) in their salad mix to small white summer turnips.

DON'T TURNIP YOUR NOSE AT THIS

White summer turnips taste nothing like their yellow winter kin. Picked when they are perhaps twice the size of radishes, they are nicely crunchy and have some of the radish taste (they are members of the same, very large, plant family) but are more delicate in flavour.

Seaview Game Farm

For years, voyagers up the Island Highway have stopped to sample chef Michel Rabu's cuisine at the Gourmet by the Sea restaurant. At the same time, lovers of torch singing have made pilgrimages to hear chanteuse Joelle Rabu at concerts around North America. So

Fallow deer and cattle at Seaview Game Farm.

it's a surprise—though not a big one—to find Michel at the helm of SEAVIEW GAME FARM (1392 Seaview Road, from either Miracle Beach Drive or Williams Beach Road, off the North Island Highway, 250-337-5182). It's a very big surprise to find Joelle welcoming visitors when she's not on tour.

Seaview is on 68 hectares that have been farmed for more than 20 years. Only in the last few years have Michel and partner Paul Plegher converted a more conventional farm into an agritourism operation that welcomes tour groups and individuals. The casual passerby can buy farm produce, salsa, pesto, pâté, Caesar salad kits, fallow deer venison, chicken, lamb, baked goods and coffee at the farm market. "You can shop for your whole dinner here," says Joelle.

Those with more time and a desire to see what makes a farm operate can, for a small fee, tour the operations, visit the petting farm and picnic on the grounds. Seaview also has summer day camps in English or French, overnight camping in a tipi village, farm barbecues and, from November through March, cooking classes. The shop is open daily; call ahead in winter and for farm tours; visit the Website at *www.seaviewgamefarm.com* for more information.

Along the Way: The Northern Gulf Islands

Just offshore from the east coast between Qualicum Bay and Campbell River are a scattering of islands in the Gulf of Georgia where life definitely takes on a relaxed demeanour.

DENMAN ISLAND is a short ferry ride from Buckley Bay, south of Courtenay. Mainly rural, the island offers a pleasant landscape of farm fields, old farmhouses and scattered forest. You may find farm stands along the byways in season; keep your eyes open for signs. Apple Lane Orchards (250-335-0296) and East Cider Orchard (250-335-2294) have cider and eating varieties of heirloom apples. Check also for a Saturday morning market that may be operating.

Across Lambert Channel by ferry is HORNBY ISLAND, long home to free spirits and artists of all varieties. The Hornby market is on Wednesdays and Saturdays, at a relaxed time of 11 a.m. to 2 p.m., behind the Community Hall. Depending on season and inclination, you may find farm and garden stands along the roads. The main farm attraction on this island, though, is the seven-hectare ELDERFIELD OLD-TIME FARM (Northwind Trail, off Strachan Road off Central Road; 250-335-2570; last Friday in June through last Friday in August, 11 a.m. to 3 p.m.). The farm is an open-air museum that takes visitors through the farming past and introduces them to present-day rural life. The Bevan/Lebaron family is the original homestead family here, clearing crown land they bought in the early 1970s. Though they do use some modern farm equipment, where possible they work by hand with antique tools, hearkening back to a simpler farming era. Happy to be subsistence farmers, they sell or trade surplus eggs and other products to neighbours.

For a small admission fee, visitors can see barnyard demonstrations and take part in goat grooming, egg-gathering and other farmyard tasks. Group reservations are available in June and September; for more information, check the Website at *www.hornbyisland.com/elderfield*.

To the north, across Discovery Passage from Campbell River, is QUADRA ISLAND. Quadra has a Saturday morning market, occasional farm stands along the road, and a chance to experience farm life at BOLD POINT FARMSTAY (Heriot Bay, 250-285-2272). This four-hectare organic farm offers guests the chance to take part in pesticide-free gardening and natural animal care, plus activities such as pickling, canning and smoking.

On CORTES ISLAND, the most distant of the Gulf Islands reachable by ferry, keep an eye out for roadside stands offering surplus produce.

index

about the author

Author photo: Gary Green

Rosemary Neering can't think of a better way to spend a sunny Vancouver Island afternoon than trundling around farm country, sampling strawberries and exotic lettuces and baby turnips and figs and a dozen varieties of apples and cheese and wine and...well, anything that's on the farm stands or in the farm markets on any given day. She's bought at the farmgate everywhere she has lived or travelled, and thinks Vancouver Island is one of the most rewarding regions anywhere for farmgaters.

She is the author of a number of books on Vancouver Island and British Columbia, including *Backroading Vancouver Island, Down the Road: Journeys through Small-Town British Columbia* and *Wild West Women: Travellers, Adventurers and Rebels;* a frequent contributor to *British Columbia Magazine;* and a past contributor to *Northwest Best Places.*

She lives in Victoria, BC, with her partner, Joe Thompson, and her cat, Cayambe.